And God said,
Let there be Light: and
there became Light.

The Reality of Revelation Unveiled

Advantage™
INSPIRATIONAL

MICHAEL A. RILES

The Reality of Revelation, Unveiled by Michael A. Riles
Copyright © 2013 by Michael A. Riles
All Rights Reserved.
ISBN 978-1-59755-141-0

Published by: ADVANTAGE BOOKS™
                www.advbookstore.com

This book and parts thereof may not be reproduced in any form, stored in a retrieval system or transmitted in any form by any means (electronic, mechanical, photocopy, recording or otherwise) without prior written permission of the author, except as provided by United States of America copyright law.

Scripture quotations are taken from The Holy Bible, King James Version (KJV).

Library of Congress Control Number: 2012922179

Cover design by Pat Theriault

First Printing: February 2013
13 14 15 16 17 18 19   10 9 8 7 6 5 4
Printed in the United States of America

Acknowledgements

Primarily giving all praise and thanks to my LORD and to my Savior Christ Yasha`yah, to whom I am so grateful. There are no words to describe the true peace and blessings that come through having a personal relationship with God.

To all my brothers and sisters who follow and obey God's word in truth; thank you all for making this journey and this endeavor worthwhile.

The Reality of Revelation, Unveiled

Table of Contents

Acknowledgements 3

Introduction 7

Chapter 1: Introduction of the Coming of Christ 9

Chapter 2: The Message of the Messiah to the Apostate Church 17

Chapter 3: The Key of David 29

Chapter 4: The Vision of a Throne 39

Chapter 5: The Anointed of Judah Prevails to Loosen the Seals 45

Chapter 6: The Six Seals Opened 51

Chapter 7: The Number of the Sealed 59

Chapter 8: The Seventh Seal 67

Chapter 9: A Star Falls from Heaven 73

Chapter 10: The Book Eaten 83

Chapter 11: The Two Witnesses 89

Chapter 12: The Red Dragon 99

Chapter 13: The Image of the Two Beasts 107

Chapter 14: The Number of the Sealed 115

Chapter 15: The Seven Angels with the Seven Last Plagues 123

Chapter 16: The Seven Vials of Wrath 127

Chapter 17: The End of the Dominion of Sin 135

Chapter 18: The Fall of Babylon 143

Chapter 19: The Marriage of the Lamb 153

Chapter 20: The Millennium 161

Chapter 21: The Description of the Heavenly Jerusalem… 167

Chapter 22: The Conclusion of the Tree of Life 177

Biography 185

Introduction

The word *apocalypse* comes from the Greek meaning "divine revelation;" hence, the revelation of Christ Yasha`yah, which unveils to the world the end of this second earth age (2 Peter 3).

The book of Revelation is unique among the other books of the Bible with its vivid descriptions and details of what will come to pass of this world age and the people therein. Our Heavenly Father YHVH does not use monstrosities as a scare tactic, but uses symbols and metaphors to convey to His children the things which are to come in the future. Like a father teaching his young child the letters in the alphabet, God YHVH uses symbols in verse to enhance our spiritual growth.

To the serious students of the Bible, I recommend turning to the Strong's Concordance Bible Dictionary to verify my findings in this manuscript, as well as the documentation in the original 1611 King James translation. The Strong's Concordance embraces the Greek, Hebrew, and Chaldean languages from which the original manuscript, the Massorah, was translated. Through my careful interpretation of the book of Revelation, and through ones similarly passionate research and study of the same, God's Word will be seen more clearly by all who choose to follow in His righteous path.

In today's world there is a reluctance of many preachers and teachers to reveal this book's true meaning chapter by chapter and verse by verse. This matter attests to the famine for hearing our Father's holy words in these end times (Am. 8:11-13). However, true followers of God shall find the truth in conscientious studying and believing.

In closing, I must confess to the belief of many who feel that the church is under attack. Nonetheless, Christ Yasha`yah teaches His followers to bear witness with action to His testimony, teaching His

Word in truth to the people of the world. Let us pray together for the new, holy Jerusalem, and the return of our Heavenly Father YHVH.

Chapter 1

Introduction of the Coming of Christ

People on Earth

¹The Revelation of Jesus Christ, which God gave unto Him, to show unto His servants things which must shortly come to pass; and He sent and signified it by His angel unto His servant John:

The unveiling of the Word of God, Christ Yasha`yah (YHVH's Savior), which God YHVH gave to Him, to show to His elect servants things that will immediately take place; and Christ Yasha`yah sent and revealed it through His angel messenger to His elect servant John:

The letters *Y H V H* (LORD) are emphatic and hidden secretly, locked five times in the acrostics in Esther 1:20, 5:4, 5:13, 7:5 and Psalms 96:11. Also locked in the acrostics in Esther 7:7 is the name *Ha Yah* (I Am, He is). The letters YHVH form the sacred name of God in the Hebrew manuscript, the Massorah. Our Father's sacred name is locked in the acrostics for the true Bible scholar to know, wherein it cannot be changed. Thus, His works are for His elect servants to see and understand His will and plan of salvation.

The term *Massorah* means "to deliver something into the

hand of another," so as to commit it to his trust without changing the thought. Therefore, God's elect servants are to listen closely and take heed to what said the Lord. *{John 5:43; Am. 3:6-8; Isa. 43:10-12; Rom. 8:14-17; Gal. 4:1-7}*

²Who bare record of the Word of God, and of the testimony of Jesus Christ, and of all things that he saw.

Who testified to the Word of God in truth, and to the testimony of Christ Yasha`yah, and whatsoever things he heard and witnessed. *{2 Pet. 1:20-21; John 1:5-7}*

³Blessed is he that readeth, and they that hear the words of this prophecy, and keep those things which are written therein: for the time is at hand.

Blessed is the one who reads diligently and those who hear with spiritual understanding the words of this prophecy, heeding those things having been written in it: indeed the time is now. *{Pro. 1:2-7; Jer. 17:7-8; Isa. 27:1-13}*

⁴John to the seven churches which are in Asia: Grace be unto you, and peace, from Him Which is, and Which was, and Which is to come; and from the seven Spirits which are before His throne;

John declaring to the seven churches in Asia: Unmerited favor and wholeness be to you from God YHVH, Who is with us now spiritually, and was with us in the first heaven and earth age, and will dwell with us de jure forevermore; and from the seven Spirits who are before His throne;

These churches represent the church bodies around the world

today which were established as major institutions of religious influence. *{3 John 1:2-3}*

⁵And from Jesus Christ, Who is the faithful Witness, and the First Begotten of the dead, and the Prince of the kings of the earth. Unto Him That loved us, and washed us from our sins in His own blood,

Even from Christ Yasha`yah, the faithful Witness, the First Begotten Son of God to conquer death, and the Shepherd of the elect servants of God. To Christ Yasha`yah who loves us and loosed us from our sins by His bloodshed on the cross, *{Col. 1:15-20; Heb. 1:6, 2:14-15; Rom. 8:28-29; John 1:1-5}*

⁶And hath made us kings and priests unto God and His Father; to Him be glory and dominion for ever and ever. Amen.

And has made the elect servants a kingdom and a royal priesthood to His God and Father YHVH; to Him be the glory and the dominion forever, even the Amen. *{Mat. 5:3-12, 13:31-33, 44-52; 1 Pet. 2:5, 9; Isa. 61:6; Ex. 19:5-6; Phn. 2:5-11}*

⁷Behold, He cometh with clouds; and every eye shall see Him, and they also which pierced Him: and all kindreds of the earth shall wail because of Him. Even so, Amen.

Observe, Christ Yasha`yah is coming with hosts of angels at the Second Advent; and everyone will witness Him, including those who pierced Him: and the biblically illiterate people of the world will wail on account of Him. Of a truth, so be it. *{Acts 1:9-11; 1 Ths. 4:15-18; John 8:44, 19:34; Zec. 12:10, 13:6; Mat. 24:30; Heb. 12:1}*

⁸I am Alpha and Omega, the beginning and the ending, saith the LORD, Which is, and Which was, and Which is to come, the Almighty.

I Am that I Am, the Beginning (of life) and the End (of death), said God YHVH, Who is with us now spiritually, was with us in the first heaven and earth age, and will dwell de jure on earth for ages to come, the Almighty.

"I Am that I Am" is *HaYah asher HaYah* in the Hebrew language, being all-conclusive; thus saying, I will be what I will be or become, the Eternal. *{Heb. 11:6; Col. 1:18; Ex. 3:13-15; 2 Pet. 3:5-7; Isa. 44:6-8, 46:9-10; Luk. 20:38}*

⁹I John, who also am your brother, and companion in tribulation, and in the kingdom and patience of Jesus Christ, was in the isle that is called Patmos, for the word of God and for the testimony of Jesus Christ.

I, John, your brother and fellow-partaker in the tribulation, as well as with this kingdom and perseverance in Christ Yasha`yah, was placed on the island of Patmos, because of the Word of God and the testimony of Christ Yasha`yah. *{Rom. 5:1-5}*

¹⁰I was in the Spirit on the Lord's Day, and heard behind me a great voice, as of a trumpet,

I came to be under the power of the Spirit in the Day of the Lord Christ, and I heard behind me a loud voice like the sound of a war trumpet,

The Day of the Lord is the first day of the millennium. The trumpet is connected with war, and the victory of the thousand-year reign in Christ. {2 Ths. 2:2-3; 2 Pet. 3:8-10; Zep. 1:14-16; Isa. 2:12, 61:2, 63:4}

[11] Saying, I am Alpha and Omega, the first and the last: and what thou seest, write in a book, and send it unto the seven churches which are in Asia; unto Ephesus, and unto Smyrna, and unto Pergamos, and unto Thyatira, and unto Sardis, and unto Philadelphia, and unto Laodicea.

Saying, I Am the Eternal: and what you witness, write in a book, and send it to the many-membered church body.

Seven in biblical numeric denotes spiritual perfection or completeness. The seven churches represent the many-membered church body in general that John is to write. Only the remnant, representing God's elect servants, has the seal to understand the Word of God in truth and in depth by the Holy Spirit through the prophets of old. {Isa. 1:9; Am. 3:7-8; John 14:21-27, 17:8-22; Mat. 5:29-30; Rom. 11:4-8, 12:4-5}

[12] And I turned to see the voice that spake with me. And being turned, I saw seven golden candlesticks;

And I turned to see the speaker who was speaking with me. And in turning, I saw seven churches; {Rev. 1:20}

[13] And in the midst of the seven candlesticks one like unto the Son of Man, clothed with a garment down to the foot, and girt about the paps with a golden girdle.

And in the midst of the many-membered church body was Christ Yasha`yah, arrayed in His righteous acts garment down to

His feet, and girded across his chest with the gospel armor. {Eph. 6:14-15; Isa. 11:1-5}

¹⁴His head and His hairs were white like wool, as white as snow; and His eyes were as a flame of fire;

And the hairs on His head were white as lamb's wool, being pure as snow; and His Shekhinah Glory (appearance) was as a consuming fire;

The lamb's wool symbolizes Christ Yasha`yah as our faithful Shepherd and the perfect Lamb sacrifice for all of mankind's sins upon repentance. The white snow symbolizes His holiness and sacredness. The flame represents His Holy Spirit of truth, as the eyes are the mirrors to the soul. {Deu. 4:24; Heb. 12:29; 2 Co. 3:17; Dan. 7:9, 10:5-6}

¹⁵And His feet like unto fine brass, as if they burned in a furnace; and His voice as the sound of many waters.

And the feet of Him were like burnished bronze, as glowing in a furnace; and His voice as the roar of a mass of people.

Christ's voice is thunderous for all to hear with understanding and clarity, and his feet are as burning bronze to tread down all evil elements. {Ex. 9:28; 2 Sam. 22:14; Isa. 63:3; Psa. 108:13; Eze. 1:26-28, 43:2; Rev. 17:15}

¹⁶And He had in His right hand seven stars: and out of His mouth went a sharp twoedged sword: and His countenance was as the sun shineth in his strength.

And holding in His right hand of power seven angel

Chapter 1: Introduction of the Coming of Christ

messengers of God: and out of His mouth flowed forth the living Word of God: and His express image was the Divine favor and effulgence of God's Shekhinah glory.

The seven angel messengers also represent the seven thousand of God's elect servants, which exhibit an efficient amount in which He utilizes to carry out His glorious will and plan of salvation. *{Rom. 11:4-5; Zec. 3:9; Heb. 1:3, 4:12; John 8:12, 10:27-29; Isa. 11:4; Rev. 1:20}*

¹⁷*And when I saw Him, I fell at His feet as dead. And He laid his right hand upon me, saying unto me, Fear not; I am the First and Last:*

And when I saw Him, I fell at His feet paralyzed in amazement. And He placed His right hand upon me, saying, Do not be afraid; for I Am the First and the Last of the ways, and works, and Word of God:

Love and reverence Christ our Lord; do not be scared of Him. *{Deu. 6:4-9; Isa. 12:2-6, 41:4}*

¹⁸ *I am He That liveth, and was dead; and, behold, I am alive for evermore, Amen; and have the keys of hell and of death.*

I am the Living One, Who was crucified; and, behold, Living am I forevermore, of a truth; and I have the keys of death and of hell.

Christ the victor has the keys to unlock one's mind of all things that keep one in bondage and hell bound. Therefore, one must study diligently to show himself approved, and have faith with works in order to receive the blessings and inheritance of eternal life. *{1 Pet. 3:18-20; Col. 2:14-15; 2 Tim. 1:10; Luk. 16:22-31; Jer. 10:10; 1 Co. 15:55-57; Psa. 49:15; Mat. 16:19}*

¹⁹ Write the things which thou hast seen, and the things which are, and the things which shall be hereafter;

Write therefore the things that you have seen, what they signify, even the things that are about to occur after these things; *{Isa. 46:9-10}*

²⁰ The mystery of the seven stars which thou sawest in My right hand, and the seven golden candlesticks. The seven stars are the angels of the seven churches: and the seven candlesticks which thou sawest are the seven churches.

As for the secret symbol of the seven stars which you saw in My right hand of power, and the seven golden candlesticks. The seven stars signify the angel messengers to the seven churches: and the seven candlesticks signify the seven churches.

The seven stars also represent the seven thousand elect servants of God, which He utilizes in these end times to witness and teach His Word in truth to the people of the world. God YHVH intercedes in the elect lives because they overcame in the first heaven and earth age, having fought against the dragon Satan. They were therefore predestined and judged, and thus glorified in the first heaven and earth age. *{Zec. 4:2; Rom. 8:27-31, 10:13-15, 11:4-8; Rev. 12:7-9}*

Chapter 2

The Message of the Messiah to the Apostate Church

People on Earth

¹Unto the angel of the church of Ephesus write; These things saith He That holdeth the seven stars in His right hand, Who walketh in the midst of the seven golden candlesticks;

To the angel of the church in Ephesus write; These things said Christ Yasha`yah, Who possesses the seven angels of God in His right hand of power, and Who walks in the midst of the many-membered church body; {Mat. 18:20; Rom. 12:4-5; Lev. 26:11-12}

²I know thy works, and thy labour and thy patience, and how thou canst not bear them which are evil, and thou hast tried them which say they are apostles, and are not, and hast found them liars:

I know your works, toil, perseverance, and how you cannot tolerate evil men working mischief, having examined those calling themselves apostles of God, and they are not, but have found them erroneous: {Isa. 66:18; Mar. 13:5-6; Rom. 2:7; 2 Co. 11:10-15}

³And hast borne, and hast patience, and for My name's sake hast laboured, and hast not fainted.

And has persevered, and has endured for My name's sake, and has not grown weary. *{Heb. 12:3; Mar. 13:13}*

⁴Nevertheless I have somewhat against thee, because thou hast left thy first love.

Nevertheless I have this against you, that you have forsaken your first love, the Word of God in truth.

Unfortunately, many churches today are guilty of this because they have allowed religion, theories and traditions of men to replace God's impeccable and holy Word. *{Ex. 20:1-6; Deu. 7:7-10; Mat. 15:8-9}*

⁵Remember therefore from whence thou art fallen, and repent, and do the first works; or else I will come unto thee quickly, and will remove thy candlestick out of His place, except thou repent.

Therefore consider where you have fallen under condemnation, and be transformed by the renewing of your mind and do the deeds you did at first; if not, I will visit you, and will remove your church from My many-membered body, unless you repent. *{Zec. 8:16-17; Mat. 4:17, 6:33; Deu. 30:1-3; Lev. 26:40-42}*

⁶But this thou hast, that thou hatest the deeds of the Nicolaitanes, which I also hate.

But this you have in your favor: that you hate the deeds of the Nicolaitanes, which I also hate.

The Nicolaitanes were Baal worshipers and idolaters of a heretical sect who were hateful towards God and never stood up for righteousness.

⁷*He that hath an ear, let him hear what the Spirit saith unto the churches; To him that overcometh will I give to eat of the tree of life, which is in the midst of the Paradise of God.*

He who listens diligently, let him understand what the Holy Spirit is saying concerning the churches; To him that overcomes the prince of the world Satan, I will give to partake of the tree of life Christ, which is in the Paradise of God YHVH. *{John 16:33; Gen. 3:22; Zec. 6:15; Eze. 47:12; Rev. 22:1-5, 14-17}*

⁸*And unto the angel of the church in Smyrna write; These things saith the First and the Last, Which was dead, and is alive;*

And to the angel of the church in Smyrna write; These things said Christ Yasha`yah, Who died, and lived again;

Christ defeated the prince of death Satan by dying on the cross as the perfect Lamb sacrifice for all mankind to enter into immortality on repentance. *{Gen. 3:14-15; Acts 4:9-12; 1 Co. 15:54-57; Heb. 2:9-15}*

⁹*I know thy works, and tribulation, and poverty (but thou art rich), and I know the blasphemy of them which say they are Jews, and are not, but are the synagogue of Satan.*

I know your tribulation and poverty (but you are rich in Me

with spiritual gifts and eternal treasures), and I know the slander of the Kenites, who claim to be of the king-line tribe of Judah, and are not, but are the house of Satan.

The Kenites are the sons of Cain, and Cain is the offspring of Satan the devil. This is why one can never document or find Cain in the genealogy of the man Adam in the entire bible or the history of this world. Satan is symbolized as the serpent and as the tree of the perception of good and evil from the Garden of Eden. In history, the Kenites were vagabonds and resided in the land of Judea among the Israelites. During this time, the Kenites took over the liturgical duties of the Levites as the priests and scribes of God's holy Word, and throughout history have made subtle changes to the Holy Scriptures to endorse their specific objectives. Because the Kenites lived in the land of Judea among the tribe of Judah, they began to call themselves Jews, and erroneously do so to this day. The king-line tribe of Judah and Levi are the tribes which Christ would come through in the flesh as YHVH's Savior (Yasha'yah).

Satan's method of operation is subtlety, perception, and deception. Satan uses great deception to promote his children, the Kenites, as the true children of Israel. To claim to be a *Jew* would indicate heritage from only one tribe of Israel, Judah; but those claiming such heritage do not declare their association with Christ and the remaining eleven tribes. Christ told us to learn and understand the parable of the fig tree and who the good and bad figs are. *Fig leaves* denote covered or things hidden. The good figs are the true Israelites which are hidden in the world today, because they are the scattered and lost tribes who have been dismantled and robbed of their heritage and identity. The bad figs are the Kenites whose true identity as the biological children of Satan is hidden by their false claim of Jewry heritage.

CHAPTER 2: THE MESSAGE OF THE MESSIAH TO THE APOSTATE CHURCH

The two churches that Christ found well pleasing are Smyrna and Philadelphia. These two churches stand apart from the others because they taught the facts of God's word and the truth about who the Kenites are. *{Deu. 28:62-68; 2 Co. 6:9-10; Mat. 13:36-43, 23:1-22; Mar. 13:28-29; Ezra 8:15-20; Num. 24:21-22; Gen. 3:7, 13-15; 1 Jn. 3:12; 1 Chr. 2:55; Eze. 31:1-18; Jer. 35:1-19; John 8:42-52, 19:36-37, 20:19}*

¹⁰Fear none of those things which thou shalt suffer: behold, the devil shall cast some of you into prison, that ye may be tried; and ye shall have tribulation ten days: be thou faithful unto death, and I will give thee a crown of life.

Do not fear what you are about to suffer: behold, Satan will betray some of you to courts and synagogues, that you may be browbeaten; and you will have tribulation ten days (within the five-month period): be faithful, even to the point of death, and I will give to you the crown of eternal life. *{Mat. 16:24-28, 24:9-10; Mar. 13:9-12, 19-23; Luk. 12:11-12; John 8:51; Rev. 9:5; 1 Pet. 5:4}*

¹¹He that hath an ear, let him hear what the Spirit saith unto the churches; He that overcometh shall not be hurt of the second death.

He who listens diligently, let him understand what the Holy Spirit is saying concerning the churches; the one overcoming Satan will not suffer the final blotting out of the soul. *{Rev. 20:14-15}*

¹²And to the angel of the church in Pergamos write; These things saith He Which hath the sharp sword with two-edges;

To the angel of the church in Pergamum write; These things said Christ Yasha`yah, Whose tongue is the true, living Word of God (that cuts both ways through lies and deception);

Pergamum was a city of Mysia famous for the heathen worship of Aesculapius, the ancient Roman god of medicine and healing, to whom the title of *savior* was given, and whose emblem was the serpent. The city was also involved in the idol worship of Apollo, one of the gods in Greek mythology. *{Heb. 4:12}*

¹³*I know thy works, and where thou dwellest, even in Jerusalem on Mount Zion where Satan's seat is: and thou holdest fast My name, and hast not denied My faith, even in those days wherein Antipas was My faithful martyr, who was slain among you, where Satan dwelleth.*

I know where you dwell, even in Jerusalem on Mount Zion where the throne of Satan as the Antichrist will be set up: and you held firm My reputation, and did not deny My faith, even in the days of Antipas, My faithful witness, who was murdered among you, where Satan dwells (spiritually).

Antipas in the Greek means "like the father," representing he who stands against the false father, Satan. *Antichrist* means "instead of Christ," and represents the other father, not the Heavenly Father YHVH. *{2 Ths. 2:1-4; Mat. 7:21-23}*

¹⁴*But I have a few things against thee, because thou hast there them that hold the doctrine of Balaam, who taught Balac to cast a stumbling block before the children of Israel, to eat things sacrificed unto idols, and to commit fornication.*

But I have a few things against you, because you have false ministers who hold the doctrine of Baal worship, and are instructed by the hierarchy to teach traditions of men for profit, casting a snare before the sons of Israel, so that they partake of things sacrificed to idols and to commit acts of immorality. *{Josh. 13:22; Deu. 30:15-20; Jer. 9:13-15; Eze. 8:13-18, 13:16-23; Num. 25:1-5, 31:16; 2 Pet. 2:15; Jud. 11}*

¹⁵So hast thou also them that hold the doctrine of the Nicolaitanes, which thing I hate.

Likewise, you also have those who in like manner hold the teaching of the Nicolaitanes. *{Rom. 1:21-32; Luk. 12:1}*

¹⁶Repent; or else I will come unto thee quickly, and will fight against them with the sword of My mouth.

Change your way of thinking, therefore! Or else, I will visit you suddenly, and will make war against your church with the truth of My mouth. *{Heb. 4:12; Isa. 55:6-9; 1 Ths. 5:2-3; Mat. 24:42-51}*

¹⁷He that hath an ear, let him hear what the Spirit saith unto the churches. To him that overcometh will I give to eat of the hidden manna, and will give him a white stone, and in the stone a new name written, which no man knoweth saving he that receiveth it.

He who listens diligently, let him understand what the Holy Spirit is saying concerning the churches. The one overcoming Satan, I will give to him the love and wisdom of God, having been mysterious, and will give him the victory Stone, and on the stone a new name written, which no one knows except he who receives it.

The white stone is known to the ancients as the victory stone, which is symbolic of Christ Yasha`yah as our Glorious Rock and Victor. The word *manna* being translated in Hebrew means "what's that?" Manna is angel's food and the blessed, and is symbolic of the truth of God's Word which is mysterious to most people in the world today. Those overcoming are given a new name as the bride of Christ. {Col. 1:26; Rev. 3:12; Ex. 16:14-15, 32-34; Deu. 8:3-6; Isa. 56:5-6, 62:2-5, 65:13; Psa. 78:24-25; 1 Co. 2:4-9, 13:9-12}

¹⁸And unto the angel of the church in Thyatira write; These things saith the Son of God, Who hath His eyes like unto a flame of fire, and His feet are like fine brass;

To the angel of the church in Thyatira write; these things said Christ Yasha`yah, whose Being is a consuming fire, and His feet are like burnished bronze (prepared for treading down in judgment);

Thyatira was a town located between Pergamos and Sardis, and was another worship center for Apollo and Artemis, the Greek mythological god and goddess. {Jer. 23:29-30; Mal. 4:2-3; Rev. 19:13-15}

¹⁹I know thy works, and charity, and service, and faith, and thy patience, and thy works; and the last to be more than the first.

I know your deeds, and your love and faith, your service and perseverance; and the latter of your deeds being greater than at first.

²⁰Notwithstanding, I have a few things against thee, because thou sufferest that woman Jezebel, which calleth herself a prophetess, to teach and to seduce My servants to commit fornication, and to eat things sacrificed unto idols.

Nevertheless, I have this against you, that you tolerate the tyrant woman Jezebel, who calls herself a prophetess of God, to teach falsehood and to seduce My bond-servants so that they commit acts of immorality and partake of idolatrous offerings.

The name *Jezebel* is symbolic of any harlot of Satan (false minister) as being a lawless one. This Jezebel, who pretended to be a prophetess, and being addicted to antinomianism, taught that Christians are freed from God's established moral law, and are merely required to rely on faith and divine grace for salvation without the righteous works of the law. Religion and denominationalism is a heretical system utilized by men and is one of the four hidden dynasties of Satan which people worship in ignorance, claiming to worship the One True God YHVH. Christianity is not a religion but a reality. *{Rom. 3:30-31; Jas. 2:8-26; Mat. 5:16-20; Ex. 34:11-16; 2 Co. 11:3-4; Mar. 13:22; 1 Jn. 4:1-6; Eze. 13:3, 16-23}*

²¹And I gave her space to repent of her fornication; and she repented not.

And I have given the religious harlot time that she might change her way of thinking; but she was not willing to repent of her immorality.

Most biblically illiterate ministers and their followers will not change from their doctrinal errors because they believe they hold the truth according to the teachings that have been passed down from religious institutions throughout the ages. They do not study in depth or research diligently and are not ever taught verse by verse by gifted teachers of God in order to discover the truth of the matter. *{Jer. 14:13-17; 2 Pet. 3:9}*

²²Behold, I will cast her into a bed, and them that commit adultery with her into great tribulation, except they repent of their deeds.

Therefore, I will cast the religious harlot on a sickbed (being afflicted with plagues), and those committing idolatry with her into great tribulation, unless they repent of her iniquities. *{Deu. 28:15-22, 62-68; Rom. 2:8-9, 16}*

²³And I will kill her children with death; and all the churches shall know that I am He Which searcheth the reins and hearts: and I will give unto every one of you according to your works.

And I will destroy her children with pestilence, and all the churches will know that I Am He who searches the affections, purposes, and innermost thoughts of the soul; and I will reward everyone according to the works he or she has done on earth.

Our Heavenly Father YHVH cannot be conned; for indeed He knows what is in the mind and soul conscience of a person. *{2 Ths. 2:9-12; Deu. 30:15-19; Jer. 11:20, 17:10, 20:12; Psa.139; Rev. 6:8, 18:8}*

²⁴But unto you I say, and unto the rest in Thyatira, as many as have not this doctrine, and which have not known the depths of Satan, as they speak; I will put upon you none other burden.

But I say to you and to the rest in Thyatira, those who do not hold this teaching and have not learned the profound secret whoredoms of Satan, as they call them; I will lay no other burden upon you.

The majority of people today are greatly deceived and are being spiritually seduced because they are misinformed in God's Word regarding the profound mysteries of Satan and how he disguises himself spiritually and physically in numerous ways and occasions. Such disguises are those as the spurious messiah Antichrist, as the serpent and tree of the perception of good and evil in the garden, as the wicked and bitter influence over the biblically illiterate people of the world, and as the false shepherds who claim to be sent forth by God to teach His holy and glorious gospel. *{Pro. 9:13-18; 2 Ths. 2:7-12; 1 Co. 10:13-14; 2 Co. 2:11; 1 Jn. 4:1-6}*

²⁵But that which ye have already, hold fast till I come.

But that which you have knowledge and understanding of in truth, hold firm until I (Christ) return.

Although the church in Thyatira was not well pleasing to Christ because of their doctrinal errors, there was a remnant within the city that understood God's Word in truth and were not deceived and seduced by Satan. Christ is speaking to that elect remnant, encouraging them to hold firm the truth despite the persecutions, popular belief, and what the unlearned masses claim and testify as truth and righteousness. *{Rom. 11:4-5}*

²⁶And he that overcometh, and keepeth My works unto

the end, to him will I give power over the nations:

He who overcomes Satan, and heeds My works in truth until the end (of this second earth age), to him I will give authority over the nations: *{Mat. 24:13; Eze. 44:27-28}*

²⁷ And he shall rule them with a rod of iron; as the vessels of a potter shall they be broken to shivers: even as I received of My Father.

And he will shepherd the nations with an iron scepter and stern discipline; and as mortal souls, they will suffer extreme sorrow and be, as it were, crushed: just as I (Christ) also have received authority from My Father. *{Psa. 2:7-12; Eze. 44:23-25; Heb. 1:8-9; Rev. 21:24-26}*

²⁸ And I will give him the morning star.

And I will give to the one overcoming the True, Bright Morning Star, Christ Yasha`yah. *{Phn. 3:20-21; Rev. 22:16; Num. 24:17; Eze. 44:28}*

²⁹ He that hath an ear, let him hear what the Spirit saith unto the churches.

He who listens diligently, let him understand what the Holy Spirit is saying concerning the churches.

Chapter 3

The Key of David

People on Earth

¹And unto the angel of the church in Sardis write; These things saith He That hath the seven Spirits of God, and the seven stars; I know thy works, that thou hast a name that thou livest, and art dead.

To the angel of the church in Sardis write; These things said Christ Yasha`yah who possesses the seven Spirits of God and the seven angel; I know your deeds, that you have a reputation of being alive, and yet you are spiritually dead.

Sardis is the ancient capital of Lydia. A massive temple was constructed by the inhabitants for the goddess Cybele who was called "the mother of the gods." *{John 4:24; Pro. 9:1-2}*

²Be watchful, and strengthen the things which remain, that are ready to die: for I have not found thy works perfect before God.

Be vigilant, and strengthen the remaining infirmities, which are about to perish; indeed I have not found your deeds well pleasing in the sight of My God. *{Mat. 24:42-44; Mar. 13:31-37; 2 Pet. 3:9-13}*

³Remember therefore how thou hast received and heard, and hold fast, and repent. If therefore thou shalt

not watch, I will come on thee as a thief, and thou shalt not know what hour I will come upon thee.

Keep in mind, therefore, what you have received and heard with understanding, and hold firm, and change your way of thinking. If you will not watch with spiritual discernment (for the signs of the times), I will come when you least expect it, and you will not know at what hour I will come to you. *{Jer. 13:16-17; 2 Ths. 2:9-12; Mar. 13:28-37; Luk. 12:37-40}*

⁴ Thou hast a few names even in Sardis which have not defiled their garments; and they shall walk with Me in white: for they are worthy.

But you have a remnant in Sardis who has not spiritually defiled their righteous acts garments; and they will fellowship with Me dressed in their fine, bright and pure linen righteous acts garment: because they are worthy.

These few of God's elect servants were not spiritually seduced because they knew and obeyed the glorious gospel of Christ in truth and not the doctrines, heresies and traditions of men. *{1 Jn. 1:5-7; Eze. 6:8-10, 14:21-23, 44:17-18; 2 Co. 7:1; Rom. 11:5}*

⁵He that overcometh, the same shall be clothed in white raiment; and I will not blot out his name out of the book of life, but I will confess his name before My Father, and before His angels.

CHAPTER 3: THE KEY OF DAVID

The one overcoming Satan will thus be dressed in a fine, bright, and pure linen righteous acts garment; and I will not erase his name from the book of eternal life, but I will celebrate that soul before My Father YHVH, and before His heavenly hosts. *{Luk. 12:8-9, 15:9-10; Mat. 10:32; Rev. 19:8; Eze. 44:17-18}*

⁶*He that hath an ear, let him hear what the Spirit saith unto the churches.*

He who listens diligently, let him understand what the Holy Spirit is saying concerning the churches.

⁷*And to the angel of the church in Philadelphia write; These things saith He That is Holy, He That is True, He That hath the key of David, He That openeth, and no man shutteth, and shutteth, and no man openeth;*

To the angel of the church in Philadelphia write; These things said Christ Yasha`yah Who is The Holy and True One having the key of David to unlock the wisdom and understanding of God's word, Who reveals, and no one can conceal, and who conceals and no one reveals;

Philadelphia is about 30 miles southeast of Sardis. Although not much is known about the city, the Greek name suggests a Macedonian population. *{Isa. 22:22-23; Hos. 11:9}*

⁸*I know thy works: behold, I have set before thee an open door, and no man can shut it: for thou hast a little strength, and hast kept My Word, and hast not denied My name.*

I know your deeds. Behold, I have given you true wisdom and

31

understanding which no one can conceal: because you have a little knowledge, and heed My Word in truth, and have persevered in confessing My Holy reputation.
{1 Co. 2:6-10}

⁹Behold, I will make them of the synagogue of Satan, which say they are Jews, and are not, but do lie; behold, I will make them to come and worship before thy feet, and to know that I have loved thee.

Behold, I will cause the Kenites of the house of Satan, who declare themselves to be of the king-line tribe of Judah, and are not, but do lie; behold, I will compel them to come and worship at your feet (on the Day of the Lord), and they will know that I have loved you.

Teaching the truth of who the Kenites are is what sets the churches of Philadelphia and Smyrna apart from the other five churches. This calculates to only 28.5 percent of churches being well pleasing to God YHVH and Christ the Messiah. *{Isa. 60:14; John 8:43-55, 14:21; Mat. 23:2-9; Luk. 20:46-47; Rev. 2:9; 1 Chr. 2:55; Jer. 35}*

¹⁰Because thou hast kept the Word of My patience, I also will keep thee from the hour of temptation, which shall come upon all the world, to try them that dwell upon the earth.

Because you know and obey the Word of My perseverance, I will also guard you from being spiritually seduced during the five-month period of the Antichrist's reign, which is about to come upon the whole inhabited world, to test the people dwelling upon the earth.

Chapter 3: The Key of David

The hour of temptation has been reduced to a five-month period from a three-and-a-half-year period. These five months are May through September, representing the fig tree and locust seasons. This period will be to prove and test the faith, knowledge, love and obedience of mankind concerning our Heavenly Father YHVH's will and plan of salvation. *{Rev. 9:3-5; Deu. 13:1-8; Zep. 1:14-18; Mar. 13:19-23}*

¹¹*Behold, I come quickly: hold that fast which thou hast, that no man take thy crown.*

I am coming suddenly. Hold firm My testimony that you have, so that no one will take your crown of eternal life. *{Mar. 13:5-6; Jas. 1:12; 2 Ths. 1:8-12; Mal. 3:5; Zec. 9:16}*

¹²*Him that overcometh will I make a pillar in the Temple of My God, and he shall go no more out: and I will write upon him the name of My God, and the name of the city of My God, which is new Jerusalem, which cometh down out of heaven from My God: and I will write upon him My new name.*

To the one overcoming Satan will I make a minister who will uphold the kingdom and righteousness of My God YHVH, and he will not at all go out anymore to fight: and I will write on the tablets of his mind the name of My God, and the name of the city of My God, the new Jerusalem, which will descend from heaven from My God, and My new name.

When the bride gets married, her name changes to the groom's. *{Pro. 7:1-3; Isa. 60:13-14, 62:2-4, 65:15; Eze. 48:35; Psa. 48:1-2, 8-9; Rev. 19:7-9, 21:2, 22}*

¹³He that hath an ear, let him hear what the Spirit saith unto the churches.

He who listens diligently, let him understand what the Holy Spirit is saying concerning the churches.

¹⁴And unto the angel of the church of the Laodiceans write; These things saith the Amen, the faithful and true Witness, the beginning of the creation of God;

And to the angel of the church of Laodicea write; These things said the Amen, Christ Yasha`yah, the faithful and true Witness, the Beginning and Chief ruler of the creation of God YHVH; *{John 1:1-5; Pro. 8:22-31; Col. 1:15-20; 2 Co. 1:20}*

¹⁵I know thy works, that thou art neither cold nor hot: I would thou wert cold or hot.

I know your deeds, that you are neither against Satan nor are you for Me: I wish you were either all for Satan (death) or be all for Me (eternal life).

To be unbelieving and indifferent is to automatically choose Satan, the prince of death. God is a consuming fire, being fervent and exhibiting loving kindness, grace and compassion, while Satan is cold-hearted and exhibits cruelty and bitterness. *{Deu. 30:19-20; Ecc. 9:10; Mat. 6:24}*

¹⁶So then because thou art lukewarm, and neither cold nor hot, I will spue thee out of My mouth.

Therefore because you are indifferent, being neither against Satan nor being for Me, I will reject you with extreme disgust from

CHAPTER 3: THE KEY OF DAVID

My many-membered body.

Christ Yasha`yah will spit out as waste the names of those who are indifferent or atheists, and will not confess nor celebrate them before God YHVH and the angels. *{Isa. 19:14; Zep. 1:12; Jas. 1:7-8; Mat. 7:21-23}*

¹⁷Because thou sayest, I am rich, and increased with goods, and have need of nothing; and knowest not that thou art wretched, and miserable, and poor, and blind, and naked:

For you say, I am wealthy, and abounding in material resources, and have no need of Salvation (Yasha`yah); and do not realize that you are of the wretched one (Satan), miserable, destitute of the Christian virtues and the eternal riches (spiritually poor), and biblically illiterate (spiritually blind), with no righteous acts (spiritually naked):

The Laodiceans had success in banking, trade, and commerce, but their spiritual lives yielded low spiritual dividends. Because they were so highly motivated concerning material wealth, they lacked real spiritual commitment for wise prioritizing. *{Hos. 2:11-12, 5:15; Zec. 11:4-5; Mat. 6:19-21; Rom. 7:24-25; 2 Pet. 1:3-11}*

¹⁸I counsel thee to buy of Me gold tried in the fire, that thou mayest be rich; and white raiment, that thou mayest be clothed, and that the shame of thy nakedness do not appear; and anoint thine eyes with eyesalve, that thou mayest see.

I counsel you to buy from Me fruits of righteousness having

been refined by the Holy Spirit, so that you may be eternally rich with spiritual gifts and blessings; and righteous acts, so that you may be armored with the gospel and your indecent (lewd) acts be not revealed; and anoint your eyes with spiritual wisdom and knowledge, that you may see with understanding God's will and plan of Salvation. *{Isa. 9:6, 28:29, 55:1-3; Pro. 23:23; 1 Co. 2:9-16, 3:12-13, 12:7-11; Zec. 13:9; 1 Pet. 1:7-9}*

¹⁹*As many as I love, I rebuke and chasten: be zealous therefore, and repent.*

Those whom I love, I reprove and discipline; therefore be earnest in the pursuit of good, and change your way of thinking. *{2 Pet. 1:2-11; Heb. 12:5-11; John 16:8-11}*

²⁰*Behold, I stand at the door, and knock: if any man hear My voice, and open the door, I will come in to him, and will sup with him, and he with Me.*

Behold, I have taken My position, and speak of excellent things (inviting whomsoever will to the wedding feast): if anyone will hear My testimony with understanding, and open the door of his mind, I will come in to him and share deep truth with him, and he with Me. *{Mat. 26:26-30; Pro. 8:4-12; Rev. 19:9; Luk. 12:35-38; 1 Co. 2:9}*

²¹*To him that overcometh will I grant to sit with Me in My throne, even as I also overcame, and am set down with My Father in His throne.*

To the one overcoming Satan, I will grant him to sit with Me on My throne, as I also overcame and sat down on the right hand side of My Father on His throne. *{Heb. 1:2-3; Luk. 22:26-30; John*

12:26, 16:33; Eph. 1:20-21}

²²He that hath an ear, let him hear what the Spirit saith unto the churches.

He who listens diligently, let him understand what the Holy Spirit is saying concerning the churches.

THE REALITY OF REVELATION, UNVEILED

Chapter 4

The Vision of a Throne

In Heaven

¹After this I looked, and behold, a door was opened in heaven: and the first voice which I heard was as it were of a trumpet talking with me, which said, Come up hither, and I will shew thee things which must be hereafter.

After these things, I (John) saw a door standing open in the kingdom of heaven: and the Lord's voice that I heard was like a war trumpet emitting a sound, saying, Come up here, and I will show you what is absolutely necessary to take place in the final days and thereafter.

John is under the power of Holy Spirit on the Lord's Day to witness what will soon happen to the people who are here on earth in the last days just before Christ's Second Advent. *{Rev. 1:10; Isa. 42:9}*

²And immediately I was in the Spirit: and behold, a throne was set in heaven, and One sat on the throne.

And immediately I came to be in heaven by the power of the Spirit: and behold, a throne was set in heaven, and God YHVH was sitting on the throne. *{Eze. 1:26-28}*

³And He That sat was to look upon like a jasper and a sardine stone: and there was a rainbow round about the throne, in sight like unto an emerald.

And God YHVH that was sitting had an appearance like a jasper and sardius stone: and there was a beautiful prism of light encircling the throne, in appearance like to an emerald.

The sardius and the jasper stone represent the first and last precious stones in the breastplate of the Levitical high priest, as well as our Glorious Rock of Ages. *{Gen. 9:13; Deu. 32:4; Eze. 1:28; Ex. 28:17-21}*

⁴And round about the throne were four and twenty seats: and upon the seats I saw four and twenty elders sitting, clothed in white raiment; and they had on their heads crowns of gold.

And around the throne of God were twenty-four thrones: and on the thrones I saw twenty-four elders sitting, arrayed in their righteous acts garments; and they had crowns of victory on their heads.

The crowns of victory represent the triumph over Satan and the receipt of righteous rewards from our gracious Heavenly Father YHVH. *{Rev. 14:4, 19:8-9; 1 Chr. 24:2-5}*

⁵And out of the throne proceeded lightnings and thunderings and voices: and there were seven lamps of fire burning before the throne, which are the seven Spirits of God.

CHAPTER 4: THE VISION OF A THRONE

Out from the heavenly throne proceeded flashes of lightning, and the rumbling voices of Elohim (God) and voices. And there were seven messengers of truth before God's throne, representing the seven Spirits of God. *{Ex. 19:16-19; Job 37:1-5; Zec. 3:8-9; John 5:35, 12:28-30; Rev. 1:4, 5:6}*

⁶And before the throne there was a sea of glass like unto crystal: and in the midst of the throne, and round about the throne, were four beasts full of eyes before and behind.

And before the throne was the Holy of Holies. And in the midst of, and surrounding the mercy seat of God, were four living creatures full of knowledge and guarding the throne of God YHVH. *{Gen. 3:24; Ex. 25:17-22; Heb. 9:5; Eze. 1:5-14}*

⁷And the first beast was like a lion, and the second beast like a calf, and the third beast had a face as a man, and the fourth beast was like a flying eagle.

And the first living creature was like a young lion, faced in an eastward direction; and the second living creature was like an ox, faced in a westward direction; and the third living creature had the face of a man, faced in a southward direction; and the fourth living creature was like an eagle, faced in a northward direction.

The first living creature characterizes Christ Yasha`yah as a lion being a brave and mighty hero, and represents the king-line tribe of Judah. The second living creature characterizes Christ Yasha`yah as being the Faithful and True Witness of God, plowing through the carnal minds of the people, and represents the tribe of Ephraim. The third living creature characterizes Christ Yasha`yah as the only Begotten Son and Savior of God YHVH in the flesh through the root of David, and represents the tribe of Reuben, which in Hebrew means "to behold a son." The fourth living creature characterizes Christ Yasha`yah as an eagle, being our refuge, fortress, and judge, and represents the tribe of Dan, which in Hebrew means "judge."

These entities embody some of the characteristics of Christ Yasha`yah, who is the standard of Israel and all who follow Him. *{Eze. 1:4-11; Num. 2:2-3, 10, 18, 25}*

⁸And the four beasts had each of them six wings about him; and they were full of eyes within: and they rest not day and night, saying, Holy, holy, holy, LORD God Almighty, Which was, and is, and is to come.

And the four living creatures having respectively six wings, guarded the mercy seat of God YHVH; and they were full of knowledge and insight: and they incessantly say, Holy, holy, holy, YHVH God Almighty, Who is the same yesterday, today, and forever.

These four living creature guards were created without free will to give praise and glory to the Heavenly Father continually. Conversely, the cherub Satan, who also guarded the mercy seat of God in the first heaven and earth age, was given free will. Satan fell from grace for being lawless, unruly and prideful towards God, desiring to take over His position and mercy seat. Because of his iniquities and pride, Satan was cast down as profane and condemned and sentenced to perish for eternity as the only son of perdition. *{Ex. 25:17-22; Eze. 28:14-19; Isa. 6:3, 14:12-19; Heb. 13:7-8}*

⁹And when those beasts give glory and honour and

thanks to Him That sat on the throne, Who liveth for ever and ever,

And whenever the four living creatures give glory, honor, and thanksgiving to God YHVH, Who is the Eternal, *{Eze. 1:4-14}*

¹⁰The four and twenty elders fall down before Him That sat on the throne, and worship Him That liveth for ever and ever, and cast their crowns before the throne, saying,

The twenty-four elders fall prostrate before Him, and worship Him Who is the Eternal, and cast their crowns of victory before the throne, saying,

¹¹Thou art worthy, O LORD, to receive glory and honour and power: for Thou hast created all things, and for Thy pleasure they are and were created.

Worthy are You, YHVH our God, to receive all the glory, the honor, and the authority: for You created all things, and for Your pleasure they existed and were created. *{Isa. 43:7-11, 45:11-12; Col. 1:16-17; Psa. 103:21}*

The Reality of Revelation, Unveiled

Chapter 5

The Anointed of Judah Prevails to Loosen the Seals

In Heaven

¹And I saw in the right hand of Him That sat on the throne a book written within and on the backside, sealed with seven seals.

I, John, saw in the right hand of God YHVH Who sits on the throne, a Bible having been written all-inclusively and sealed spiritually with seven seals (whereby it could not be disclosed).

²And I saw a strong angel proclaiming with a loud voice, Who is worthy to open the book, and to loose the seals thereof?

And I witnessed a mighty angel proclaiming with authority, "Who is worthy to unseal the Bible, and to unveil the spiritual wisdom, knowledge, and understanding therein?"

The more diligently a person researches and studies the scriptures, the more seals will be removed from their mind, and they can know and understand with clarity God's Word in truth.

³And no man in heaven, nor in earth, neither under the earth, was able to open the book, neither to look thereon.

And no living soul in heaven, or human being on earth, neither mortal soul in the abyss, was able to unseal the Bible, neither spiritually understand the perfect and finished works of God therein. *{1 Co. 2:6-15; 2 Co. 4:3-7; Isa. 29:9-12}*

⁴And I wept much, because no man was found worthy to open and to read the book, neither to look thereon.

And I cried loudly, because no one was found worthy to unseal the Bible, neither spiritually discern it.

No human being is perfect or possesses all wisdom and knowledge, which is the reason for the shortcomings and incomprehension of the wisdom and knowledge written in God's Holy Word. Man's righteousness is as filthy rags compared to the Heavenly Father. Moreover, any truth, righteousness, and wisdom that we as humans possess come from God YHVH through His Holy Spirit and glorious gospel. *{Pro. 8:20-36; 20:24, 28:5; Isa. 29:10-13}*

⁵And one of the elders saith unto me, Weep not: behold, the Lion of the tribe of Judah, the Root of David, hath prevailed to open the book, and to loose the seven seals thereof.

Then one of the elders said to me, Do not weep: behold, the Brave and Mighty Hero, Christ Yasha`yah, from the king-line tribe of Judah, the Root of David (through the flesh), has prevailed at Calvary to disclose the perfect and finished works of God therein. *{Pro. 1:5-7, 2:4-11; Isa. 61:1-3; Gen. 49:8-10; John 14:23-27}*

⁶And I beheld, and lo, in the midst of the throne and of the four beasts, and in the midst of the elders, stood a

Lamb as it had been slain, having seven horns and seven eyes, which are the seven Spirits of God sent forth into all the earth.

And I saw in the midst of the throne, encircled by the four living creatures and the elders, Christ Yasha`yah standing as He had been crucified, having omnipotence and seven witnesses, which are the seven Spirits of God sent out into all the world.

The seven eyes also represent the seven thousand of God's elect servants that are sealed and utilized by way of His Holy Spirit to witness and teach His will and plan of salvation to the world. *{Phn. 2:5-11; Rom. 16:25-27; Zec. 3:8-9; Pro. 8:13-14; Mat. 28:18-20; John 14:26, 21:15}*

⁷And He came and took the book out of the right hand of Him that sat upon the throne.

And Christ Yasha`yah came and took the Bible from out of the right hand of God YHVH Who sits on the throne.

Christ Yasha`yah was able to take the book of love, truth, and righteousness, and disclose the perfect and finished works of God therein, because He is the perfect Word and Truth of God, Who was made flesh and walked the earth as YHVH's Savior. *{Mat. 12:17-21, 17:5; Eph. 3:16-21; Heb. 10:7; Psa. 40:7}*

⁸And when He had taken the book, the four beasts and four and twenty elders fell down before the Lamb, having every one of them harps, and golden vials full of odours, which are the prayers of saints.

And when He had taken the Bible, the four living creatures

and the twenty-four elders fell prostrate before Him, each one holding a harp and golden bowls full of incense smoke, which symbolizes the prayers of the saints.

Our prayers are protected and guarded for God YHVH. *{Lev. 16:12-13}*

⁹And they sung a new song, saying, Thou art worthy to take the book, and to open the seals thereof: for Thou wast slain, and hast redeemed us to God by Thy blood out of every kindred, and tongue, and people, and nation;

And they were singing a new song, saying, Worthy are You to take the Bible and disclose the perfect and finished works of God therein; because You were crucified, and have purchased for God with Your bloodshed elect men from every tribe, language, and nation; *{John 17:5-12; 1 Co. 2:7-11; Rom. 8:27-39}*

¹⁰And hast made us unto our God kings and priests, and we shall reign on the earth.

And have made them to be a kingdom and a royal priesthood to serve our God YHVH, and they will reign with Him on earth forever. *{Heb. 12:28; 1 Pet. 2:9; Eze. 44:28-31}*

¹¹And I beheld, and I heard the voice of many angels round about the throne and the beasts and the elders; and the number of them was ten thousand times ten thousand, and thousands of thousands;

And I looked, and I heard the voices of the heavenly hosts surrounding the throne of God and the four living creatures and the elders; and the number of them was innumerable;

The heavenly hosts of God include those overcoming Satan in the end times, and those who died obeying and believing in Christ prior to the tribulation of Satan as the spurious messiah Antichrist. {Ecc. 12:6-7; Dan. 7:9-10; 2 Co. 5:6-10}

¹²Saying with a loud voice, Worthy is the Lamb That was slain to receive power, and riches, and wisdom, and strength, and honour, and glory, and blessing.

Shouting, Worthy is Christ Yasha`yah who was crucified to receive the (1) power, and (2) riches, and (3) wisdom, and (4) strength, and (5) honor, and (6) glory, and (7) blessing!

Seven in biblical numeric denotes spiritual completeness. Christ Yasha`yah is complete, possessing all seven of these Spirits which He sends to the world. Today, one can possess these privileges and responsibilities that go along with being in Christ, if that person will obey, love, and do the will of God in truth.

¹³And every creature which is in heaven, and on the earth, and under the earth, and such as are in the sea, and all that are in them, heard I saying, Blessing, and honour, and glory, and power, be unto Him That sitteth upon the throne, and unto the Lamb for ever and ever.

And I heard every created thing saying, The blessing, the honor, the glory, and the dominion, is to God YHVH Who sits on the throne, and to Christ Yasha`yah forever. {Col. 3:1-4; 1 Pet. 3:21-22; Isa. 9:6-7, 45:22-23; Rom. 14:11-12}

¹⁴And the four beasts said, Amen. And the four and

twenty elders fell down and worshipped Him That liveth for ever and ever.

And the four living creatures kept saying, So let be it; and the twenty-four elders fell prostrate and worshiped the Eternal Father, God YHVH. *{Jer. 10:10-12}*

Chapter 6

The Six Seals Opened

On Earth

¹And I saw when the Lamb opened one of the seals, and I heard, as it were the noise of thunder, one of the four beasts saying, Come and see.

And I (John) watched when Christ Yasha`yah opened one of the seven seals, and I heard one of the four living creatures saying as with a voice of thunder, Come!

²And I saw, and behold, a white horse: and he that sat on him had a bow; and a crown was given unto him: and he went forth conquering, and to conquer.

And I looked and beheld a powerful, religious spurious messiah, Satan, disguised as Christ the Messiah: and he that possessed this religious influence had a bow of fabrication (to whitewash the truth of God); and authority to rule was given to him: and he went forth conquering with religion (using traditions, myths and damnable heresies) so that he might conquer the world.

This first seal reveals that Satan is coming first as the spurious messiah Antichrist, disguised as Christ the Messiah. The color white in this verse signifies Satan's disguise as being an angel of light, and the horse symbolizes power. This white horse is not to be identified with the horse and rider in Revelation 19:11; but here is the beginning of the series of terrible judgments. The bow utilized by Satan is his weapon of false truth, traditions, deception, and religion, to spiritually seduce mankind, whitewash the facts of God's Holy Word of Salvation, and to war with the election. *{2 pet. 2:1-3; 2 Co. 11:14-15; Eph. 6:11-18; 2 Ths. 2:3-12; Mat. 24:4-5; Mar. 8:36-38, 13:5-6; Hos. 4:1-6; Eze. 13:16-21}*

³And when He had opened the second seal, I heard the second beast say, Come and see.

And when Christ Yasha`yah opened the second seal, I heard the second living creature say, Come.

⁴And there went out another horse that was red: and power was given to him that sat thereon to take peace from the earth, and that they should kill one another: and there was given unto him a great sword.

And another evil influence went forth as the war entity Satan: and it was granted to him to take the peace from the earth (through war and commotions), in order that the inhabitants on earth should slaughter one another: and to him was endued a mighty sword of lies and deception. *{Mar. 13:7; Mat. 24:5-7; 2 Ths. 2:10-12; Zec. 11:8-9}*

⁵And when He had opened the third seal, I heard the third beast say, Come and see. And I beheld, and lo, a black horse; and he that sat on him had a pair of balances in his hand.

And when Christ Yasha`yah opened the third seal, I heard the third living creature saying, Come. And I looked and beheld the

Famine entity Satan, which brought forth a famine in the land for hearing the Word of God in truth; and Satan, had a fixed, imbalanced system under his authority.

Satan uses his balances of deceit and bias to outweigh the justice, political, and economic systems. The economic and political systems represent two of the four hidden dynasties of the world. {Eze. 28:2-7, 16-18; Hos. 12:7-8; Mar. 13:8; Am. 8:1-13; Lam. 4:4-8; Deu. 28:29-30; Isa. 8:20-22}

⁶And I heard a voice in the midst of the four beasts say, A measure of wheat for a penny, and three measures of barley for a penny; and see thou hurt not the oil and the wine.

And I heard a voice in the midst of the four living creatures warning, A famine is in the land for receiving the bread of life (the truth of God's Word); touch not God's anointed, and act not contrary to those with the truth.

Bread by weight indicates ration and scarcity, showing the famine for the bread of life (truth) in these end times. God's elect were called, judged, and chosen in the first earth age, being predestined as God's anointed ones to witness and bring forth the true teachings of God's Word in these famine end times. The olive oil *(el-ah'-yah* in Hebrew*)* is the anointing oil of God YHVH, and the wine represents the blood (pure truth) of the Anointed One, Christ Yasha`yah, through which all can live eternally upon repentance. {Mat. 24:7; Mar. 13:8; Rom. 8:26-31; Psa. 105:15-16; Eze. 4:10, 16-17; Zec. 2:8-9, 13:8-9; Eph. 1}

⁷And when He had opened the fourth seal, I heard the voice of the fourth beast say, Come and see.

And when Christ Yasha`yah opened the fourth seal, I heard the voice of the fourth living creature say, Come.

⁸And I looked, and behold, a pale horse: and his name that sat on him was Death, and Hell followed with him. And power was given unto them over the fourth part of the earth, to kill with the sword, and with hunger, and with death, and with the beasts of the earth.

And I looked and beheld a pallid entity: and his name is Satan, the Prince of Death, and the grave (abyss) accompanied him as his attendant. And authority was given to the four wicked entities over the whole world, to destroy with the sword of lies and deception, with famine for hearing the Word of God in truth, with death by pestilence, and by way of the four hidden dynasties (beast system) of the world. *{Dan. 7; Mat. 24:7-8; Jer. 24:7-10; Heb. 2:14}*

⁹And when He had opened the fifth seal, I saw under the altar the souls of them that were slain for the Word of God, and for the testimony, which they held:

And when Christ Yasha`yah opened the fifth seal, I witnessed under the altar of God the souls of the elect servants who had been murdered because of the word of God, and because of the testimony of Christ in truth, which they had upheld:

This verse documents that the souls of God's children return to heaven after death, not remaining in an earthly grave. *{Ecc. 12:7; Eph. 1:1-14; Mar. 13:9-23; Mat. 5:11-12, 24:8-28; John 15:20-21; 1 Ths. 4:12-18}*

¹⁰And they cried with a loud voice, saying, How long, O Lord, holy and true, dost Thou not judge and avenge our blood on them that dwell on the earth?

Chapter 6: The Six Seals Opened

And they cried out with a loud voice, saying, How long, The Holy and True Messiah, until the Day of Judgement, when You avenge our blood upon our adversaries that inhabit the earth? *{Gen. 4:10; Dan. 12:8-13; Joe. 2:27-31; Deu. 32:43}*

[11] And white robes were given unto every one of them; and it was said unto them, that they should rest yet for a little season, until their fellowservants also and their brethren, that should be killed as they were, should be fulfilled.

And pure linen righteous acts garments were given to each one of them; and it was said to them that they should rest for a time and a season, until the act is fulfilled that their fellow elect brothers, the two anointed witnesses, are put to death even as they had been. *{Mar. 13:9-23; John 14:2-4; Rev. 11:7-12}*

[12] And I beheld when He had opened the sixth seal, and, lo, there was a great earthquake; and the sun became black as sackcloth of hair, and the moon became as blood;

And I saw when Christ opened the sixth seal, and the powers of heaven began to shake, causing a mighty earthquake; and the sun became eclipsed, and the full moon became dark as blood;

These signs immediately precede the Advent of Revelation 19. Matthew 24 covers exactly the period of the six seals. *{Gen. 1:14; Mar. 13:24-27; Mat. 24:29-30; Joe. 2:31; Luk. 21:25-27; Hag. 1:7}*

[13] And the stars of heaven fell unto the earth, even as a fig tree casteth her untimely figs, when she is shaken of a mighty wind.

And Satan and his fallen angels were cast down from heaven to the earth (by Michael the archangel), like a fig tree that casts its unripe figs out of season, when shaken by a mighty wind. *{2 Thes.2:7-14; Isa. 34:2-4; Mar. 13:18-28; Dan. 8:10; Rev. 12:7-9}*

¹⁴*And the heaven departed as a scroll when it is rolled together; and every mountain and island were moved out of their places.*

And the firmament parted asunder like a scroll rolling itself up; and every nation and small country were removed out of their places.

After this is fulfilled, the seventh seal is opened and Christ Yasha`yah descends from heaven with all of His heavenly hosts, stepping foot onto earth at the Mount of Olives as the King of kings and Lord of lords. The millennium reign of Christ and His elect then begins. *{Gen. 1:8; Mar. 13:26-27; Isa. 34:4, 40:4-5; Zec. 14:3-4; 1 Ths. 4:16-17}*

¹⁵*And the kings of the earth, and the great men, and rich men, and the chief captains, and the mighty men, and every bondman, and every free man, hid themselves in the dens and in the rocks of the mountains;*

And all of the biblically illiterate people of the world, regardless of their status in life, hid themselves in the caves and among the rocks of the mountains;

These people hid because of their embarrassment and shame of being spiritually seduced into serving and worshiping the spurious messiah Antichrist, losing their salvation, and having to then face the true Messiah, Christ Yasha`yah. Once the true Christ descends from heaven in His Shekhinah glory and all behold Him, the people intuitively become aware of their infamy and iniquities. *{Isa. 2:10-21; Luk. 21:26-27}*

¹⁶And said to the mountains and rocks, Fall on us, and hide us from the face of Him that sitteth on the throne, and from the wrath of the Lamb:

And they said to the mountains and to the rocks, Fall on us and hide us from the presence of Christ Yasha`yah, and from His judicial wrath and destruction: *{Hos. 10:8; Am. 5:18-20; Luk. 23:28-31; 2 Ths. 1:7-10}*

¹⁷For the great day of His wrath is come; and who shall be able to stand?

For the great day of His judicial wrath has come, and who is able to stand?

Only God's elect and those that have the seal of God's truth in their minds, not aiding or being deceived by Satan's lies and disguise as the Christ of God, are able to prevail and triumph. *{Joe. 2:11; Mat. 7:13-14; Luk. 13:23-28, 21:34-36; Mar. 13:20-23; 2 Pet. 1:10; Rev. 7:4}*

THE REALITY OF REVELATION, UNVEILED

Chapter 7

The Number of the Sealed

On Earth

¹And after these things I saw four angels standing on the four corners of the earth, holding the four winds of the earth, that the wind should not blow on the earth, nor on the sea, nor on any tree.

After this I saw four angels of God standing on the four corners of the earth, restraining the four spirits of fire, so that the fervent heat would not destroy the inhabited earth or anything therein. {2 Pet. 3:5-10; Dan. 7:2; Eze. 37:9; Zec. 6:5; Mar. 13:27; Jer. 49:36}

²And I saw another angel ascending from the east, having the seal of the living God: and he cried with a loud voice to the four angels, to whom it was given to hurt the earth and the sea,

And I witnessed another angel having ascended from the rising of the sun as the True Morning Star, possessing the seal of the Living God YHVH: and He shouted with a mighty voice to the four angels to whom power had been given to consummate the end of this second heaven and earth age,

This angel is the fifth angel that John witnesses. *Five* in biblical numeric denotes "grace," signifying this angel as the grace angel Christ Yasha`yah. The significance of the angel ascending from the sunrise characterizes Christ as our True Bright Morning Star and Light of the world. *{Mat. 13:40-43; Eze. 37:9, 43:1-2}*

³Saying, Hurt not the earth, neither the sea, nor the trees, till we have sealed the servants of our God in their foreheads.

Saying, Destroy not the inhabited earth or anything therein, until we have sealed the truth of God's word into the minds of His elect servants.

This seal of God's truth and wisdom is obvious and protects the elect servants and blessed ones during the tribulation of the Antichrist, marking them off as the true worshipers of the True Living God YHVH. *{Joe. 2:28-32; Eze. 37:1-10; Mat. 24:31}*

⁴And I heard the number of them which were sealed: and there were sealed an hundred and forty and four thousand of all the tribes of the children of Israel.

And I heard the number of those who were sealed with the truth of God's word in their minds: and there were sealed one hundred forty-four thousand from every tribe of the sons of Israel.

These children of Israel represent the second elect group that are preordained and will receive the seal of God through the testimony of the seven thousand of God's very elect group. The very elect group understands and teaches all of the Word of God in truth, chapter by chapter and verse by verse, today. The second elect group will come to life spiritually through the witnessing of God's very elect group, when they are offered up to the judgment places and in the synagogues to witness and testify against the Antichrist as the Holy Spirit of God speaks through them with clarity. This event takes place on the day of Pentecost during the sixth seal when Satan reigns de facto on earth as the Antichrist. *{Acts. 2:1-11; Eze. 48:11; Mar. 13:10-11; Rev. 14:3; Rom. 11:4-8, 26-29}*

⁵Of the tribe Judah were sealed twelve thousand. Of the tribe of Reuben were sealed twelve thousand. Of the tribe of Gad were sealed twelve thousand.

Twelve thousand from the tribe of Judah (representing the king-line tribe of Christ), twelve thousand from the tribe of Reuben, and twelve thousand from the tribe of Gad were sealed with the truth of God. *{Gen. 49:8-10}*

⁶Of the tribe of Aser were sealed twelve thousand. Of the tribe of Nephthalim were sealed twelve thousand. Of the tribe of Manasses were sealed twelve thousand.

Twelve thousand from the tribe of Asher, twelve thousand from the tribe of Nephthalim, and twelve thousand from the tribe of Manasseh were sealed with the truth of God. *{Num. 16:5-10}*

⁷Of the tribe of Simeon were sealed twelve thousand. Of the tribe of Levi were sealed twelve thousand. Of the tribe of Issachar were sealed twelve thousand.

Twelve thousand from the tribe of Simeon, twelve thousand from the tribe of Levi (the priest-line tribe of Israel), and twelve thousand from the tribe of Issachar were sealed with the truth of God.

⁸Of the tribe of Zabulon were sealed twelve thousand. Of the tribe of Joseph were sealed twelve thousand. Of the tribe of Benjamin were sealed twelve thousand.

Twelve thousand from the tribe of Zebulun, twelve thousand from the tribe of Joseph, and twelve thousand from the tribe of Benjamin were sealed with the truth of God.

The tribes of Dan and Ephraim were omitted because of idolatry, but they will return in the millennium after the restoration. The tribes of Levi and Joseph took the places of these two tribes. *{Gen. 49:17; Judg. 18:28-31; Lev. 24:10-16; Deu. 29:18-21; Rev. 21:12-13}*

The Vision of the Great Multitude in Heaven

⁹After this I beheld, and, lo, a great multitude, which no man could number, of all nations, and kindreds, and people, and tongues, stood before the throne, and before the Lamb, clothed with white robes, and palms in their hands;

After these things I looked, and beheld a host of people of all nationalities, which could not be numbered, standing before the throne and before Christ Yasha`yah, clothed in their pure linen righteous acts garments, with palm branches in their hands;

The host of people represents our ancestors who died hitherto obeying the laws of God and believing in Christ, and those that are converted to Christ during the tribulation of the Antichrist. The palm branch symbolizes the peace and the victory of the faithful over the adversaries of God. All who overcome Satan and the world are in heaven at this time celebrating and rejoicing with the victory as the bride adoring her King, Christ Yasha`yah. {Lev. 23:40; John 12:12-13, 16:33}

¹⁰And cried with a loud voice, saying, Salvation to our God Which sitteth upon the throne, and unto the Lamb.

And cheered with a loud voice, saying, Salvation to our God YHVH Who sits on the throne, and to our perfect sacrificial Lamb and Savior, Christ Yasha`yah. {Mat. 21:9}

¹¹And all the angels stood round about the throne, and about the elders and the four beasts, and fell before the throne on their faces, and worshipped God,

And all the angels, and the elders, and the four living creatures, stood around the throne, and they fell prostrate before the throne and worshiped God YHVH, {Deu. 6:4-6; Ex. 20:3-6}

¹²Saying, Amen: Blessing, and glory, and wisdom, and thanksgiving, and honour, and power, and might, be unto our God for ever and ever. Amen.

Saying, of a truth: (1) The blessing, (2) the glory, (3) the wisdom, (4) the thanksgiving, (5) the honor, (6) the power, and (7) the strength, are unto our God YHVH forever. So let it be.

Riches listed in Revelation 5:12 is replaced with *thanksgiving*, because God has the riches already, and now the thanksgiving from His children. Moreover, these seven descriptions represent God YHVH as being omnipotent and spiritually complete. {Rev. 5:12}

¹³And one of the elders answered, saying unto me,

What are these which are arrayed in white robes? and whence came they?

And one of the elders asked me, saying, These who are clothed in their righteous acts garments, who are they, and where did they come from? *{Rev. 19:8}*

¹⁴*And I said unto him, Sir, thou knowest. And he said unto me, These are they which came out of great tribulation, and have washed their robes, and made them white in the blood of the Lamb.*

I said to him, My lord, you know. And he said to me, These are the people overcoming the great tribulation of the Antichrist, and they have washed their righteous acts garments (by the standing of works, not of grace), purifying them by virtue of the blood of Christ's eternal covenant. *{1 Co. 6:9-11; Jas. 5:19-20; Eph. 5:25-27; Heb. 13:20-21; Rev. 20:12-13; Zec. 3:3-7; Psa. 51:2-7; Jer. 30:5-7}*

¹⁵*Therefore are they before the throne of God, and serve Him day and night in His Temple: and He That sitteth on the throne shall dwell among them.*

For this reason, they are before the throne of God YHVH, serving Him continually in His holy Temple: and He Who sits on the throne will spread His tabernacle over them de jure on earth forever. *{Eze. 38:26-28; 48:35; Isa. 4:5-6; Zep. 3:15-17; Rev. 21:3, 22}*

¹⁶*They shall hunger no more, neither thirst any more; neither shall the sun light on them, nor any heat.*

They will never hunger again, nor thirst anymore for His truth and righteousness; neither will the rays of the sun beat down upon them, nor any scorching heat.

In an angelic body people are immune to hot sun rays and scorching heat. This also symbolizes that we will no longer suffer the flesh life experiences of illness, calamity, hardship, evil, or death. *{Deu. 8:3; Isa. 30:26, 49:10-11; Rev. 21:23}*

¹⁷*For the Lamb which is in the midst of the throne shall feed them, and shall lead them unto living fountains of waters: and God shall wipe away all tears from their eyes.*

Indeed, Christ Yasha`yah, Who is in the center of the throne, will shepherd them and will guide them to fountains of waters of life: and God YHVH will wipe away every tear from their eyes.

Sadness and tears will cease to exist when the Heavenly Father blots out all the wicked elements and things that offend, and there is peace on earth forever. *{Isa. 49:8-10; Eze. 47:1-12; John 4:10-14, 14:6; 2 Pet. 3:10; Rev. 21:4, 22:1-5}*

The Reality of Revelation, Unveiled

Chapter 8

The Seventh Seal

In Heaven

¹And when he had opened the seventh seal, there was silence in heaven about the space of half an hour.

And when Christ Yasha`yah opened the final seal, there came to be silence in the heaven for about half an hour (during the hour of temptation).

The seventh seal contains the series of the seven trumpets and the series of the seven vials. Christ's return immediately ensues once these terrible judgments are fulfilled. The silence is a result of the peace in heaven after Satan as the Antichrist and his fallen angels are cast out onto the earth for the hour of temptation. *{Mar. 13:17-26; 2 Ths. 9-12; Rev. 8:7-11:14, 12:9-12, 16:1-18:24}*

²And I saw the seven angels which stood before God; and to them were given seven trumpets.

And I saw the seven angels standing before God's throne; and seven trumpets were given to them.

The trumpet is a symbol of considerable consequence. Its sounding denotes action and warning of the wrath to follow. *{Num. 10:9}*

³And another angel came and stood at the altar, having a golden censer; and there was given unto him much incense, that he should offer it with the prayers of all saints upon the golden altar which was before the throne.

And an eighth angel appeared and stood at the altar of God YHVH, holding a golden censer; and much incense was given to him, so that he would offer it with the prayers of all the saints upon the holy altar which is before the throne (mercy seat). *{Heb. 9:23-24; John 16:23; Rev. 5:8, 6:9}*

⁴And the smoke of the incense, which came with the prayers of the saints, ascended up before God out of the angel's hand.

And the smoke of the incense, with the prayers of the saints, went up before God YHVH out of the angel's hand.

⁵And the angel took the censer, and filled it with fire of the altar, and cast it into the earth: and there were voices, and thunderings, and lightnings, and an earthquake.

Then the angel took the censer, and filled it with the fire of the altar of God, and cast it to the earth: and there came to be voices, the rumbling voices of God, flashes of lightning, and an earthquake (which caused the biblically illiterate people of the world to stumble spiritually).

The shaking by the indignation and judgment of God is to awaken the unsuspecting and biblically illiterate, spiritually dead souls and enemies of God - which are sorely lacking the wisdom and knowledge of His will and plan of salvation - before the day He executes vengeance upon them. *{2 Sam. 22:14; Mic. 5:15; 1 Pet. 2:8}*

The Seven Angels with Trumpets On Earth

⁶And the seven angels which had the seven trumpets prepared themselves to sound.

And the seven angels of God that had the seven trumpets prepared themselves to execute the command.

⁷The first angel sounded, and there followed hail and fire mingled with blood, and they were cast upon the earth: and the third part of trees was burnt up, and all green grass was burnt up.

The first angel sounded his trumpet, and there came hailstones and God's righteous indignation mixed with spiritual death, and it was cast to the earth: and the third part of the supposed upright ones and the heretical, religious workers of iniquity on earth died spiritually (because of deception and confusion).

The trees and grass are symbolic of the so-called prudent and heretical religious people that are without Christ's righteous fruits and morals. They are burned by the Holy Spirit and truth of God, the consuming fire, due to their dead works and idolatry. The Holy Spirit warms and comforts the hearts of His elect servants and those who obey, but burns, offends, and shames the enemies and workers of iniquity. *{Jer. 2:13, 23:21-32; Ex. 9:18-27; Mal. 4:1; Psa. 37:1-2; 1 Co. 3:11-20, 2 Co. 11:13-15; Eze. 20:47-49; Mat. 7:15-19; 1 Jn. 2:18-23; Rev. 9:3-4, 12:4}*

⁸And the second angel sounded, and as it were a great mountain burning with fire was cast into the sea: and the third part of the sea became blood;

And the second angel sounded his trumpet, and the locust army, as it were a great nation consuming with strong delusion (the fiery darts of Satan), was cast into the sea of people on earth: and the third part of the laypeople of the world became spiritually dead (from deception);

Mountains are symbolic of nations. The locust army, which includes the Kenites nation, fallen angels, workers of iniquity, and the false religious priests of the world, is of the great city Babylon, which is Satan's state and realm of mass confusion. The laypeople of the world are those who have no goal in knowing the love of God YHVH and His plan of salvation. They do not consider themselves as believers or nonbelievers, but indifferent. *{Jer. 51:6, 24-25; Joe. 1:2-7, 2:1-10; 2 Ths. 2:7-12; Mat. 23:31-36; Rev. 9:3, 17:15, 18}*

⁹And the third part of the creatures which were in the sea, and had life, died; and the third part of the ships were destroyed.

And the third part of the mortal beings that were of the multitude and had living souls in the flesh, died spiritually (from deception); and the third part of Satan's vessels of commerce perished.

Satan's vessels of commerce represent the four hidden dynasties of the world - education, politics, economics and religion - and are utilized to manipulate and influence the world through perceptions and subliminal messages by way of advertisements, services, and paid announcements via the internet, radio, television, and other means. *{Eze. 5:2-12, 18:23-26; Dan. 4:14-17; Rev. 5:13, 18:17-19; Isa. 29:9-15; Mat. 24:4}*

[10] And the third angel sounded, and there fell a great star from heaven, burning as it were a lamp, and it fell upon the third part of the rivers, and upon the fountains of waters;

And the third angel sounded his trumpet, and there fell the false morning star Lucifer from heaven, glowing as the false light of the world: and he fell upon the third part of the supposed preachers and people of the Christian communities (those claiming to only believe and just be saved in Christ without any true knowledge of salvation and righteous acts).

The Christian communities represent those who claim to believe in and worship the one true God YHVH, but are seduced spiritually by false ministers disguised as apostles of God and Christ, heretical doctrines, and traditions and theories of men. The Heavenly Father YHVH begins His judgment at the top with the preachers and teachers, and works His way down to the laypeople. Indeed, Christianity is not a religion but is a reality. *{Mat. 7:21-24; Jer. 17:13; Eze. 9:3-6, 28:14-19, 31:4-7; Isa. 14:12-14; 2 Co. 11:13-15; Luk. 10:18}*

[11] And the name of the star is called Wormwood: and the third part of the waters became wormwood; and many men died of the waters, because they were made bitter.

And the name of the false morning star is called Bitterness: and the third part of the people became bitter; and a large part of mankind died spiritually, because they were made bitter (due to the famine of hearing God's wisdom and knowledge taught in truth, chapter by chapter and verse by verse). *{Mat. 7:21-23; 1 Pet. 5:8-9; Jer. 9:13-16, 23:15-17; Am. 8:11-13; Isa. 14:15-17; Hos. 4:1-6}*

¹²And the fourth angel sounded, and the third part of the sun was smitten, and the third part of the moon, and the third part of the stars; so as the third part of them was darkened, and the day shone not for a third part of it, and the night likewise.

And the fourth angel sounded his trumpet, and a third of the sun, moon, and stars were struck, so that a third of them should be darkened, and the day should not appear for a third of it, and likewise the night. *{Gen. 1:14; Mat. 24:29; Mar. 13:24; Joe. 2:10, 30-31; Isa. 5:30, 13:10; Zep. 1:14-18}*

¹³And I beheld, and heard an angel flying through the midst of heaven, saying with a loud voice, Woe, woe, woe, to the inhabiters of the earth by reason of the other voices of the trumpet of the three angels, which are yet to sound!

And I looked, and heard the Great Eagle of the Lord flying in mid-heaven, warning with a piercing voice, saying, Woe, woe, woe, to the people dwelling on earth because of the remaining blasts of the trumpet of the three angels of God, who are about to sound!

These three woes represent the fifth, sixth, and seventh trumpets, being characterized as the cries of an eagle. The warning is for the people that are spiritually asleep, deceived, and not under our Heavenly Father YHVH's protective wings of His will and plan of salvation. *{Deu. 32:11-12; Isa. 40:31}*

Chapter 9

A Star Falls from Heaven

On Earth

¹And the fifth angel sounded, and I saw a star fall from heaven unto the earth: and to him was given the key of the bottomless pit.

And the fifth angel sounded his trumpet, the first woe, and I witnessed the false morning star Lucifer, who had fallen from heaven to the earth: and Michael, the mighty archangel, was given the key of the pit of the abyss.

This fallen star represents Satan as the anointed cherub who was overthrown and cast down to a state of degradation in the first heaven and earth age, when iniquity and pride entered his mind, and he attempted to take over the mercy seat of The Most High, God YHVH. Satan earned his title of Antichrist because of this rebellion. The bottomless pit signifies the never-ending sins of Satan, and is the place where he dwells de facto while he is imprisoned. *{Isa. 14:12; Eze. 28:12-19; Luk. 10:18; Rev. 12:7-9, 20:1; 2 Ths. 2:7-8}*

²And he opened the bottomless pit; and there arose a smoke out of the pit, as the smoke of a great furnace; and the sun and the air were darkened by reason of the smoke of the pit.

And Michael, the mighty archangel, opened the pit of the abyss;

and there arose a great evil spirit of lies, deception, and confusion, as the smoke of a great furnace covering the whole world; and the reality of God's Word and His Holy Spirit were overshadowed by the strong delusion of Satan from the pit of the abyss.

The smoke symbolizes the great confusion and toxic lies and deception that Satan utilizes to manipulate and whitewash the truth and righteousness of God's will and plan of salvation and the reality of the Holy Spirit. *{2 Ths. 2:7-12; Dan. 11:32-35}*

³*And there came out of the smoke locusts upon the earth: and unto them was given power, as the scorpions of the earth have power.*

And out of the strong delusion of Satan came forth to the earth an army of evil workers of iniquity disguised as prophets and ministers of God and Christ: and to them were endued great deceptive influence to inflict hurt, as the venomous scorpions of the earth have ability.

The locust army represents the Kenites, false prophets, hireling preachers, and teachers, who profess to serve and teach God's Word in truth, utilizing one verse or two out of context, but only sow iniquity, damnable heresies, confusion, hypocrisy, discord, theories, and traditions of men, causing division and bringing about great deception, fraud, and false pretenses in the church and throughout the world. *{Jer. 12:10-12; 23:20-29; 2 Co. 11:13-15; 1 Jn. 2:18- 19; Joe. 2:25-32; Isa. 7:17-19}*

⁴*And it was commanded them that they should not hurt the grass of the earth, neither any green thing, neither any tree; but only those men which have not the seal of God in their foreheads.*

And it was said to them that they should not harm the grass, neither any nature, nor any tree on earth; but only the people who do not have the seal of God's truth in their minds.

Similar to locust insects that devour vegetation and fruit in nature, these Kenites, false prophets, and hireling priests, devour the righteous fruits, truth, and morals of mankind, thus robbing one of their legal tender, and the blessings, inheritance, and eternal life of YHVH. *{Hos. 6:6-7; Gal. 5:18-24; 2 Ths. 2:9-12; Eze. 9:4-10; Joe. 1:1-20, 2:2-11, 25-32}*

⁵And to them it was given that they should not kill them, but that they should be tormented five months: and their torment was as the torment of a scorpion, when he striketh a man.

And to them it was commissioned that they should not kill the biblically illiterate people of the world, but to torment them spiritually through lies and deception for a five-month period: and their act of torment was as the torment of a venomous scorpion when it stings a man (being very painful and detrimental).

The period of locusts is five months, May thru September, which represents the hour of temptation. This period of time on a solar calendar occurs between the Passover day in April and the Feast of Tabernacles in October. *{1 Jn. 4:1; Luk. 11:11-12; Isa. 66:4-5; Mat. 7:15-23; 8:28-29; Mar. 5:5-9; Gen. 7:24, 8:3}*

⁶And in those days shall men seek death, and shall not find it; and shall desire to die, and death shall flee from them.

And during that time, the biblically illiterate people of the world will seek death, and will in nowise find it; and they will wish to die, yet death will flee from them.

These people seek death due to the torment and shame of their ignorance in being deceived in God's Word, leaving them terrified to face the judicial wrath of the true Messiah, Christ Yasha`yah, at His Second Advent. *{Heb. 2:14; Rev. 6:15-17; Jer. 8:2-3; Rom. 2:8-9}*

⁷And the shapes of the locusts were like unto horses prepared unto battle; and on their heads were as it were crowns like gold, and their faces were as the faces of men.

And the appearance of the locust army (Kenites, false prophets, and hireling ministers of Satan) was like a well-organized cavalry force having been prepared for a spiritual battle; and they exalted and disguised themselves as genuine servants of God and Christ. *{Jer. 4:29-31, 6:21-23; Jn. 10:10-13; 2 Co. 11:12-15; Dan. 11:21-24; Joe. 2:8-10}*

⁸And they had hair as the hair of women, and their teeth were as the teeth of lions.

And they in disguise portrayed themselves as being holy, humble, and righteous servants of God and Christ; but the vicious lies, traditions of men, and damnable heresies that they were preaching and teaching was ferocious and caused lives to be ripped apart.

The false prophets and hireling ministers' depiction as having the hair of women signifies them as being the harlots of Satan, having subtle, covert, and conniving ways. *{Mat. 23:1-7, 23-28; 1 Pet. 5:8-9; John 10:8-13; Joe. 1:6-7}*

Chapter 9: A Star Falls from Heaven

⁹And they had breastplates, as it were breastplates of iron; and the sound of their wings was as the sound of chariots of many horses running to battle.

And they wore breastplates, as it were iron breastplates of war; and the sound of them was as a swarm rushing into battle with humbug doctrines of influential babble.

The true priesthood of the Levites wore breastplates of leather and not of iron. The leather symbolizes the Levitical priests and elect of God as humble, righteous, and compassionate shepherds. The crowns and iron breastplates of the harlot ministers of Satan symbolize their overbearing pride and arrogance, hardheartedness, hypocrisy, and lack of compassion. *{Ex. 28:15; Mic. 3:5; Luk. 17:20-21}*

¹⁰And they had tails like unto scorpions, and there were stings in their tails: and their power was to hurt men five months.

And they had detrimental, influential tales like unto venomous scorpions, and their influential babble was in their tall tales: and their deceptive influence was to seduce the unsuspecting and biblically illiterate people for a five-month period (leading them to the Antichrist and bound for hell).

Just as scorpions sting and torment their prey, with their injected venom turning the prey's insides to mush, so are these Kenites and harlot ministers injecting their venomous tales, doctrines, and false publications around the world, leaving their victims spineless and unable to stand up and fight for God and Christ's truth and righteousness. *{Isa. 5:25-30}*

¹¹And they had a king over them, which is the angel of

the bottomless pit, whose name in the Hebrew tongue is Abaddon, but in the Greek tongue hath his name Apollyon.

And they had over them a supernatural king, the angel of the pit of the abyss Satan, whose name in the Hebrew language (Old Testament) is Destruction, and in the Greek language (New Testament) he has the name Destroyer (or Cause to perish). *{Job 26:6; Dan. 8:24-25; Jer. 4:7}*

¹²One woe is past; and behold, there come two woes more hereafter.

The first woe from the fifth angel has past; discern, there are two woes still coming after these things.

¹³And the sixth angel sounded, and I heard a voice from the four horns of the golden altar which is before God,

And the sixth angel sounded his trumpet, the second woe; and I heard a mighty voice from the four projecting extremities (in shape like a horn) of the holy altar which is before God YHVH, *{Eph. 6:11-17}*

¹⁴Saying to the sixth angel which had the trumpet, Loose the four angels which are bound in the great river Euphrates.

Saying to the sixth angel who had the sixth trumpet, Release the four wicked angels who are bound in the pit of the abyss at the great river Euphrates.

The Euphrates is connected with the judgments of the

CHAPTER 9: A STAR FALLS FROM HEAVEN

Great Day of the Lord. The river is the border between the city of Babylon (confusion) and the city of Jerusalem (peace). This symbolizes the separation of the people in the state of confusion from the elect servants with the seal of God. When Satan is released, strong delusion and confusion will be as a great flood of lies covering the earth. The four messengers in this verse represent the Kenites and harlot ministers as the locust army, the fallen angels, and their leader Satan disguised as Christ the Messiah. {Mat. 10:34-39, 24:36-39; Gen. 6:1-7; Jud. 3-6; Isa. 13:4-8; Jer. 46:4-10}

**15*And the four angels were loosed, which were prepared for an hour, and a day, and a month, and a year, for to slay the third part of men.*

And the four wicked messengers were released from the pit of the abyss, having been prepared for that fixed point of time appointed by God YHVH, so that they would inflict spiritual death on a third of mankind.

**16*And the number of the army of the horsemen were two hundred thousand thousand: and I heard the number of them.*

And the number of the locust army of the cavalry forces of Satan was great: and I heard the number of them.

**17*And thus I saw the horses in the vision, and them that sat on them, having breastplates of fire, and of jacinth, and brimstone: and the heads of the horses were as the heads of lions; and out of their mouths issued fire and smoke and brimstone.*

And I witnessed the cavalry forces of the harlot ministers of Satan in my vision, wearing fiery and hyacinth-colored breastplates (of a red color bordering on black): and these Kenites and harlot ministers with great influence and authority were like ferocious lions; and out of their sermons came vicious lies, great deception, and strong delusion.

These Kenites, false prophets, and harlot ministers of Satan, are symbolized as ferocious lions which rip and tear apart their prey and reign as king (priest) of the beasts (biblical illiterate people). They utilize their priestly authority and influence to manipulate and distribute traditions of men, myths, damnable heresies, old wives' tales, and theories from the pulpit, thus seducing from the truth the masses of the unsuspecting and naive. *{Jn. 8:41-49; 2 Ths. 2:7-12; Isa. 5:26-30; Luk. 20:46-47; Jer. 6:21-23}*

[18] By these three was the third part of men killed, by the fire, and by the smoke, and by the brimstone, which issued out of their mouths.

By these three plagues of vicious lies (fiery darts of Satan), great deception, and strong delusion, which proceeded out of their sermons, was a third of mankind deceived to their spiritual deaths.

[19] For their power is in their mouth, and in their tails: for their tails were like unto serpents, and had heads; and with them they do hurt.

Indeed, the deceptive influence of the locust army is in their sermons and in their tales: indeed, their tall tales and subtle ways are like the old serpent Satan, having tremendous influence and authority; and with them they do torment. *{Gen. 3:1-6; John 8:42-44; Jer. 8:16-17}*

CHAPTER 9: A STAR FALLS FROM HEAVEN

[20] And the rest of the men which were not killed by these plagues, yet repented not of the works of their hands, that they should not worship devils, and idols of gold, and silver, and brass, and stones, and of wood: which neither can see, nor hear, nor walk:

And the rest of the men, who were not harmed by these plagues of deception, did not repent of the works of their evil deeds, so that they would not worship demonic entities and mammon: which cannot bring one to salvation:

This worship of Satan as the spurious messiah Antichrist is worldwide during the hour of temptation, despite the divine warnings from God YHVH and His elect. The worship of these demonic entities (Satan and his fallen angels) is distinguished here from the worship of idols. *{Jer. 48:10; Mat. 13:36-42, 24:37-39; 2 Co. 11:13-15; Luk. 16:13-15; Col. 2:8}*

[21] Neither repented they of their murders, nor of their sorceries, nor of their fornication, nor of their thefts.

Neither did they repent for deceiving the people to their spiritual deaths, nor for their seductions of idolatry and religious incantations, nor for their immorality, nor for stealing the kingdom and salvation of God YHVH from the unsuspecting and biblically illiterate people. *{2 Tim. 3:12-13; Gal. 5:19-21; Psa. 115:4-8; 1 Co. 2:8-9}*

The Reality of Revelation, Unveiled

Chapter 10

THE BOOK EATEN

On Earth

¹And I saw another mighty angel come down from heaven, clothed with a cloud: and a rainbow was upon His head, and His face was as it were the sun, and His feet as pillars of fire:

And I witnessed the Angel of the Lord descending from heaven, arrayed in His Shekhinah Glory: and a halo was upon His head, and the appearance of Him was as a beautiful prism of bright lights (as the True, Bright Morning Star of the world), and the feet of Him as flames rising like columns:

The term *another* shows Him to be not one of the seven. {Rev. 4:3; Ex. 3:2; Deu. 4:24; Isa. 19:1; Mat. 24:30; Heb. 12:29}

²And He had in His hand a little book open: and He set His right foot upon the sea, and His left foot on the earth,

And He held in His right hand the Bible having been opened: and He set His right foot on the sea and His left foot on the land,

The book is sealed in chapter five, but here it is opened. The second part of this verse demonstrates the dominion that the Angel of the Lord has over all the earth and the sea of people therein.

Christ Yasha`yah, our Lord and Savior, is the Angel of the Lord. *{Eze. 2:7-10, 3:1-8; Isa. 40:22; Acts 7:49-50; Eph. 1:19-23; Rev. 5:1, 17:15}*

³And cried with a loud voice, as when a lion roareth: and when He had cried, seven thunders uttered their voices.

And shouted with a roaring voice as one having authority: and when He shouted, seven peals of thunder rumbled.

The seven peals of thunder are symbolic of the voices of Elohim (God). Just as in nature, once the thunder is heard, it indicates that the lightning, symbolized as the Antichrist's reign of five months, has already come and gone. Therefore, discern, and be not ignorant to the signs of the times and the seasons that are written in our Father's Word, the Bible; because after the seventh trumpet, it will be too late to take heed to our Father's will and plan of salvation. *{Ex. 9:28; Psa. 29; 1 Ths. 4:16-18; 2 Ths. 2:8-9}*

⁴And when the seven thunders had uttered their voices, I was about to write: and I heard a voice from heaven saying unto me, Seal up those things which the seven thunders uttered, and write them not.

And when the seven peals of thunder rumbled, I (John) was beginning to write: and I heard a voice out of heaven saying, Seal up the things which the Lord has spoken, and do not write them. *{Ex. 9:28; Luk. 10:18; Mar. 13:9-11, 32-33; 1 Co. 15:51-52; Psa. 29}*

⁵And the angel which I saw stand upon the sea and upon the earth lifted up His hand to heaven,

Chapter 10: The Book Eaten

And the Angel of the Lord whom I witnessed standing on the sea and on the land lifted up His right hand to heaven, *{Mat. 5:34-35}*

⁶And sware by Him that liveth for ever and ever, Who created heaven, and the things that therein are, and the earth, and the things that therein are, and the sea, and the things which are therein, that there should be time no longer:

And swore by the Eternal God YHVH, Who created heaven, earth, and everything therein, that there shall be no more delay in executing final vengeance:

During this time it is the Day of the Lord, representing the millennium reign of Christ and His saints when His vengeance is executed upon the enemies. *{2 Pet. 3:7-10; Isa. 45:11-12; Rev. 6:10-11}*

⁷But in the days of the voice of the seventh angel, when he shall begin to sound, the mystery of God should be finished, as He hath declared to His servants the prophets.

But in the day when the seventh angel is about to sound the seventh trumpet (the third woe), the will and plan of YHVH's salvation will have been completed also, as He proclaimed to His own servants the prophets. *{Mat. 13:34-43; Hos. 12:10; Dan. 12:1-13; Am. 3:7-8; Jer. 51}*

⁸And the voice which I heard from heaven spake unto me again, and said, Go and take the little book which is open in the hand of the angel which standeth upon the sea and upon the earth.

And the voice that I heard from heaven spoke again with me, saying, Go, take the Bible that is open in the right hand of the Angel of the Lord standing on the sea and on the land.

⁹And I went unto the angel, and said unto him, Give me the little book. And He said unto me, Take it, and eat it up; and it shall make thy belly bitter, but it shall be in thy mouth sweet as honey.

And I went to the Angel of the Lord, saying to Him, give me the Bible. And He replied, Take it (emphasizing action required), and receive the wisdom and knowledge written therein; and it will make your flesh bitter, but in your mouth will be the sweet truth of God YHVH.

Eat it up is a Hebraism for receiving knowledge. {Jas. 3:13-18; Pro. 2:6; Isa. 34:16; Eze. 2:7-10, 3:1-3}

¹⁰And I took the little book out of the angel's hand, and ate it up; and it was in my mouth sweet as honey: and as soon as I had eaten it, my belly was bitter.

And I took the Bible (bread of life) out of the Angel of the Lord's hand, and devoured the wisdom and knowledge written therein; and in my mouth it was the sweet truth of YHVH's Word: and when I had received the wisdom and knowledge, my flesh became bitter.

God's truth is bittersweet when first digested; the flesh wars against the Spirit and righteousness of God, but our spirit is made alive and vivacious by it. {Rom. 7:12-25; 8:5-10; Jer. 15:16, 29:13; Mar. 14:38; Pro. 4:4-7, 18:20; 1 Pet. 4:1-2}

CHAPTER 10: THE BOOK EATEN

¹¹And He said unto me, Thou must prophesy again before many peoples, and nations, and tongues, and kings.

And They said to me, you must prophesy and witness again concerning many peoples, nations, languages and world rulers. *{Eze. 33:1-7; Mat. 28:18-20; Mar. 16:15-20; Acts 2:16-18; Hos. 12:10}*

The Reality of Revelation, Unveiled

Chapter 11

The Two Witnesses

On Earth

¹And there was given me a reed like unto a rod: and the angel stood, saying, Rise, and measure the temple of God, and the altar, and them that worship therein.

Then there was given me (John) a measuring reed like a scepter (correction rod): and the giver said, Rise and measure (for the destruction of) the temple of God and the altar, and record the people that worship in it.

This scepter measures for the destruction and grinding of idol temples of men at Christ's Second Advent, and not for building. It separates God's elect servants who obey in truth and overcome this second world age, from Satan's workers of iniquity who defile the church of God on earth with false religion, idolatry, theories, and traditions of men, being condemned. The temple mentioned here should not be confused with the Heavenly Temple of God revealed ahead in verse nineteen.
{Mat. 24:1-2; Lam. 2:6-9; Deu. 32:16-21; Jer. 7:29-33; Hos. 6:6}

²But the court which is without the temple leave out, and measure it not; for it is given unto the Gentiles: and the holy city shall they tread under foot forty and two months.

But the court that is outside the temple leave out, and do not measure it; because it has been given to the Gentile nations: and they will make desolate the city of Jerusalem for forty-two months (which was reduced to a five-month period).

Months represent the moon or lunar and Satan and his children of the night. Whenever prophecy is given in months, Satan is involved within it. Forty-two months is a three-and-a-half year period on a moon calendar of 29.5 days per month. However, God reduced this period of desolation to a five-month period of May through September, which is the locust season naturally and spiritually. This reduced period is 147.5 days on a lunar calendar. *{Rom. 11; 2 Ths. 2:3-4; Rev. 9:5-11; Jer. 26:2-6; Mar. 13:18-20; Dan. 7:25, 9:25-27, 12:7-12}*

³And I will give power unto My two witnesses, and they shall prophesy a thousand two hundred and threescore days, clothed in sackcloth.

And I (Angel of the Lord) will grant wondrous powers to My two witnesses, and they will prophesy one thousand two hundred and sixty days (the five-month period), invested with humility.

Days represent the sun or solar, and are associated with Christ Yasha`yah and God's elect servants as the children of the light. A solar calendar contains 30.45 days within a month as opposed to the lunar calendar which contains 29.5 days per month. Whenever prophecy is given in days, it is prophesied towards God's elect children. The reduced period is 152.25 days on a solar calendar. The significance of the discrepancy between the number of lunar days Satan will reign, and the number of solar days that the two anointed witnesses are present, is prophecy within itself. The two anointed witnesses of God will be here on earth five to ten days longer than

Satan, arriving before him to testify of his coming as the Antichrist. *{1 Ths. 5:1-9; John 12:35-36; 1 Jn. 1:4-7}*

⁴These are the two olive trees and the two candlesticks, standing before the God of the earth.

These represent the two anointed witnesses and the two churches which stand before and serve God YHVH of the universe.

These two churches are Smyrna and Philadelphia, which are the two that Christ found well pleasing because of the truth that they taught about the Kenites, who claim to be of the king-line tribe of Judah (Jews), and are not, but are the house of Satan the devil. Smyrna and Philadelphia represent God's anointed and elect servants who know and teach boldly all of His Word in truth as written in the Bible. *{Zec. 4:3, 11-14; Joe. 2:28-32; Rev. 2:9, 3:8-10; Mat. 13:34-43}*

⁵And if any man will hurt them, fire proceedeth out of their mouth, and devoureth their enemies; and if any man will hurt them, he must in this manner be killed.

And if anyone should wish to harm the two anointed witnesses, lightning will proceed out from heaven by their commands, and devour their enemies. And if anyone harms them, it behooves for that individual in like manner to be put to death. *{2 Kgs. 1:10-12; Psa. 104:4; Jer. 5:12-15; Luk. 9:54}*

⁶These have power to shut heaven, that it rain not in the days of their prophecy: and have power over waters to turn them to blood, and to smite the earth with all plagues, as often as they will.

These two anointed witnesses have the authority to stop the rain from falling in the days of their prophesying (like Elijah): and have authority to turn the waters into blood (like Moses), and to smite the earth with every plague of God's wrath, as often as they desire.

Spiritually speaking, the early and latter day rains are the knowledge and wisdom of our Father's Word. The early rain causes the seed of God's Word to germinate and sprout in your mind. The latter rain of God's Word allows your mind to mature with understanding and utilize God's wisdom and knowledge, thus producing fruits of righteousness and truth to honor and serve God YHVH and Christ. *{Ex. 4:9; Isa. 5:5-6; Jer. 5:24; Zec. 10:1-2, 14:11-19}*

⁷And when they shall have finished their testimony, the beast that ascendeth out of the bottomless pit shall make war against them, and shall overcome them, and kill them:

And when they have finished their testimony, the spurious messiah Antichrist who ascends out of the pit of the abyss, will make war against them, and will overcome them, and murder them:

Once the two anointed witnesses of God finish their testimony, they will be at the mercy of their enemies and be murdered. When Satan as the Antichrist slays these two, he will have broken God's command of, "touch not Mine anointed [...]." *{Mar. 13:9-11; 1 Chr. 16:21-22; Rev. 6:11, 9:4, 17:8}*

⁸And their dead bodies shall lie in the street of the great city, which spiritually is called Sodom and Egypt, where also our Lord was crucified.

And their corpses will lie publicly in the court arena of the great city Jerusalem, which spiritually is called Perversion (Sodom) and Abomination (Egypt), where indeed their Lord Christ Yasha`yah was crucified.

The city of Jerusalem is the city of peace. However, at this time, during the abomination of the Desolator (the reign of Satan as the Antichrist), it is a city of desolation.
{Dan. 9:27; Mar. 13:14; Eze. 16:46-53; Jer. 22:8-10; Isa. 25:2-9}

⁹And they of the people and kindreds and tongues and nations shall see their dead bodies three days and a half, and shall not suffer their dead bodies to be put in graves.

And those of the peoples and tribes and languages and nations will gaze upon the dead bodies of the two anointed witnesses lying in the court arena in Jerusalem for three-and-a-half days; and the unsuspecting and nonbelievers will not permit their corpses to be laid in a tomb.

The two anointed witnesses will have great authority in utilizing their wondrous powers and the truth of God's Word, but the biblically illiterate people of the world will choose not to believe them or their testimony. Therefore, they will be left lying dead in the court in Jerusalem so that the people can witness their dead bodies to see to know if what they testified will come to pass. *{Psa. 79:1-3}*

¹⁰And they that dwell upon the earth shall rejoice over them, and make merry, and shall send gifts one to another; because these two prophets tormented them that dwelt on the earth.

And the unsuspecting and biblically illiterate people will gloat over them and celebrate by sending gifts to one another (as an expression of honor); because these two anointed witnesses tormented them dwelling upon the earth.

The biblically illiterate people of the world are tormented due to the testimony of the two anointed witnesses that the man claiming to be Christ the Messiah is really Satan as the Antichrist, disguised in order to seduce them. The masses of unlearned people who believe that Christ is coming to rapture them away will be deceived by the Antichrist who comes in peacefully, prospering everyone, solving all of the world's problems with this claim. They will assume and believe that the two anointed witnesses are against them and their newfound salvation with Satan as the Antichrist, but will soon discover that they were truly sent forth by God YHVH and Christ Yasha`yah to deliver the will and plan of true salvation. *{Eph. 6:10-18; Dan. 9:26-27, 11:21-24; Eze. 13:17-23}*

¹¹*And after three days and an half the spirit of life from God entered into them, and they stood upon their feet; and great fear fell upon them which saw them.*

But after the three-and-a-half days, the breath of life from God YHVH entered into His two anointed witnesses, and they were resurrected; and a paralyzing fear came over the unsuspecting people beholding them.

The people that rejoiced and celebrated over the murders of the two anointed witnesses, and made mockery of them, will now see and know that what they testified was true and has come to pass. *{Gen. 2:7}*

¹²*And they heard a great voice from heaven saying unto*

them, Come up hither. And they ascended up to heaven in a cloud; and their enemies beheld them.

And they heard a mighty voice from heaven saying to the two anointed witnesses, Come up here. And they ascended to heaven into the cloud of witnesses while their enemies gazed at them.

The cloud (multitude) of witnesses, also called *the gathering*, represents the angels of God, including the people who have already died, believing and serving God and Christ in truth, and gone to heaven. *{Heb. 12:1; Jud. 14-16}*

¹³*And the same hour was there a great earthquake, and the tenth part of the city fell, and in the earthquake were slain of men seven thousand: and the remnant were affrighted, and gave glory to the God of heaven.*

And in that hour of temptation a great earthquake occurred, and a tenth of the city fell; and in the earthquake, seven thousand names of men (as the fallen angels of Satan) perished: and the remaining ones, as God's elect servants, became terrified, and gave glory to God YHVH of heaven.

The city falls when Christ Yasha`yah steps foot onto earth at the Mount of Olives, causing a massive earthquake around the world. *{Gen. 6:4; Zec. 14:1-4; Jer. 10:10; Jud. 5-7; Isa. 10:20-22; Phi. 2:10; Rom. 11:4-6}*

¹⁴*The second woe is past; and behold, the third woe cometh quickly.*

The second woe (sixth trumpet) has passed; and discern, for the third woe (the seventh trumpet and final warning) is coming immediately.

The Seventh Trumpet In Heaven

¹⁵And the seventh angel sounded; and there were great voices in heaven, saying, The kingdoms of this world are become the kingdoms of our LORD, and of His Christ; and He shall reign for ever and ever.

And the seventh angel sounded his trumpet (the third woe); and there came to be fervent voices in heaven, saying, The kingdom of the world has become the sovereignty of our Heavenly Father YHVH and His Anointed One Yasha'yah; and He will reign eternally. *{Ex. 15:18; Psa. 146:10}*

¹⁶And the four and twenty elders, which sat before God on their seats, fell upon their faces, and worshipped God,

And the twenty-four elders sitting before God on His throne, fell prostrate and worshiped God YHVH,

¹⁷Saying, We give thee thanks, O LORD God Almighty, Which art, and wast, and art to come; because Thou hast taken to Thee Thy great power, and hast reigned.

Saying, we give thanks to You, YHVH God Almighty, The I Am; because You have taken Your omnipotent authority, and have come to reign.

¹⁸And the nations were angry, and Thy wrath is come, and the time of the dead that they should be judged, and that Thou shouldest give reward unto Thy servants the prophets, and to the saints, and

them that fear Thy name, small and great; and shouldest destroy them which destroy the earth.

And the deceived nations became enraged, for Your fierce wrath has come, and the time for condemning the mortal souls, and to give the divine reward of immortality to all Your chosen elect servants and those who reverence and obey You in truth; and to utterly destroy the evil entities that defile the earth. *{2 Pet. 3:10; 1 Co. 15:52-57; Rev. 2:11; 18, 19, 20; Dan. 7:18; Isa. 13:9-13, 26:20-21}*

[19] And the Temple of God was opened in heaven, and there was seen in His temple the ark of His testament: and there were lightnings, and voices, and thunderings, and an earthquake, and great hail.

And the Temple of God which is in heaven was opened, and the ark of His covenant was seen therein: and there came flashes of lightning, the rumbling voices of Elohim (God), an earthquake, and a severe hailstorm. *{Rev. 8:5, 16:21; Luk. 1:70-80; Ex. 9:28, 25:10-22}*

The Reality of Revelation, Unveiled

Chapter 12

The Red Dragon

In Heaven

¹And there appeared a great wonder in heaven; a woman clothed with the sun, and the moon under her feet, and upon her head a crown of twelve stars:

And a great sign was seen in heaven; mother Israel invested with the covenant of God as the light of the world, having authority over the prince of darkness Satan, and upon her glory the twelve zodiac signs of the heavens:

The twelve signs of the zodiac are called the *stars*, being numbered and named, representing the twelve tribes of Israel in embryo. *{Gen. 37:9; Deu. 4:1-14, 20; Eph. 3:8-11; 1 Co. 2:7-9; Mat. 19:28; Mal. 4:2-3}*

²And she being with child cried, travailing in birth, and pained to be delivered.

And she having child in the womb cried out, travailing in birth (with the third heaven and earth age), and tormented to be delivered.

This verse is symbolic of the birth of the third earth age. The third heaven and earth age, which is forth coming, will be like the first heaven and earth age before the overthrow of Satan and his rebellion, which caused the earth to become without form, and void (*tohu va bohu* in the

Hebrew language) by an immense shaking and massive flood, not speaking of Noah's flood in this second earth age. *{Psa. 119:129-130; Mat. 24:21-22; John 16:20-22; Rom. 8:19-23; 2 Pet. 3:5-7; Isa. 45:18-19; Jer. 4:23-27; Gen. 1:1-2; Mic. 5:2-4}*

³And there appeared another wonder in heaven; and behold, a great red dragon, having seven heads and the ten horns, and seven crowns upon his heads.

And another sign was seen in heaven; and I beheld the prince of this (second) world age Satan, having dominion over the seven continents (earthly powers), his ten supernatural, fallen angels, and the seven kingdoms of Jerusalem. *{Isa. 14:12, 16-18; John 14:30; Rev. 17:10}*

⁴And his tail drew the third part of the stars of heaven, and did cast them to the earth: and the dragon stood before the woman which was ready to be delivered, for to devour her child as soon as it was born.

And Satan's tall tale and deception seduced a third of God's children in heaven, causing those who followed him to be cast down from heaven to degradation: and he stands before the woman Israel who would bring forth the promised seed (Christ Yasha`yah and His elect), in order to devour when she gives birth.

Satan has made several attempts to stop God YHVH's will and plan of salvation: through Abel's murder by Cain, since through the seed line of the man Adam (*'eth-ha'adham* in Hebrew) and Eve would come Christ as the Savior; through the fallen angels mixing with the Adamic race in order to contaminate the pedigree; through Pharaoh's order to murder all the Hebrew sons born in Egypt; through King Herod's order to kill all of the children born in

Bethlehem two years of age and under; and many more.

Satan's first rebellion in the first earth age, and those who followed him, is the reason that every living soul having free will, and God's elect, must pass through this second earth age once. Christ was sent to earth as YHVH's Salvation (Yasha'yah) to enable those who did not overcome Satan's first rebellion to be saved and reunited with their Creator God YHVH. This second earth age is a time of opportunity for those who did not overcome in the first earth age, to now show and prove, and to choose whom they will reverence and serve: YHVH our Heavenly Father, or Satan the devil our adversary. *{Gen. 3:14-15, 4:8, 6:1-6; Ex. 1:15-22; Isa. 9:15; Mat. 2:12-20, 13:36-43}*

⁵And she brought forth a man child, who was to rule all nations with a rod of iron: and her child was caught up unto God, and to His throne.

And she (Mary) gave birth to the male child (Christ Yasha`yah), who will shepherd all the nations with stern discipline upon His Second Advent: and He was crucified on the cross, resurrected, and seized to God YHVH and to His throne.

The first time Christ came to earth was as our Kinsman Redeemer and Savior; but at His return, He will rule the nations with an iron scepter, and reign as the King of kings and the Lord of lords. *{Phn. 2:5-11; 1 Pet. 1:19-21; Luk. 2:23}*

⁶And the woman fled into the wilderness, where she hath a place prepared of God, that they should feed her there a thousand two hundred and threescore days.

And the twelve tribes of Israel and God's elect servants (as the bride and wife of Christ) were scattered among the Gentile nations, where they have predestination ordained by God, and where the prince of this world Satan and the nations will feed them lies and deception for one thousand two hundred and sixty days (until the end of the five-month reign of the Antichrist). *{Rev. 12:14; Deu. 28:62-68; Dan. 7:1-28; Rom. 8:26-39, 11:1-11; Eph. 1; Mar. 13:20-23; Eze. 20:33-38; 2 Co. 11:2-4}*

The War in Heaven Satan, the Deceiver of the Whole World In Heaven

⁷And there was war in heaven: Michael and his angels fought against the dragon; and the dragon fought and his angels,

And there came to be war in the heaven: Michael the mighty archangel and his righteous angels, the elect servants of God, went forth to war against the great serpent Satan; and Satan warred back with his wicked fallen angels,

⁸And prevailed not, neither was their place found any more in heaven.

But he was not strong enough, nor was found a place for them anymore in heaven. *{Jud. 6; 2 Ths. 2:7-8; Luk. 10:19; Dan. 10:13-21}*

⁹And the great dragon was cast out, that old serpent, called the devil and Satan, which deceiveth the whole world: he was cast out into the earth, and his angels were cast out with him.

And the great serpent Satan was cast down, that ancient serpent from the Garden of Eden, who is called the slanderer and the adversary, the one deceiving the whole inhabited world (except those with the seal of God's truth in their minds): he was cast down into the earth along with his evil fallen angels. *{Isa. 14:12-17; Gen. 3:1, 14-15, 6:1-5; 1 Pet. 5:8}*

¹⁰And I heard a loud voice saying in heaven, Now is come salvation, and strength, and the kingdom of our God, and the power of His Christ: for the accuser of our brethren is cast down, which accused them before our God day and night.

And I heard a mighty voice in heaven, saying, Now have come the salvation, and the power, and the kingdom of our God YHVH, and the authority of His Anointed One: because Satan, the accuser of our elect brothers was cast down, the one accusing them before our God YHVH continuously. *{Zec. 3:1-2; Job 1:6-12; Mat. 12:48-50}*

¹¹And they overcame him by the blood of the lamb, and by the word of their testimony; and they loved not their lives unto the death.

And God's elect servants overcame Satan by reason of the atonement of Christ Yasha`yah's crucifixion and by reason of the truth of their testimony; and they desired not to live their lives unto the prince of death Satan. *{John 12:24-26; Rom. 5:8-11; Heb. 2:9-17}*

¹²Therefore rejoice, ye heavens, and ye that dwell in them. Woe to the inhabiters of the earth and of the sea! for the devil is come down unto you, having great wrath, because he knoweth that he hath but a short time.

For this reason rejoice, you heavens, and you that tabernacle therein. Woe to the biblically illiterate people and the unsuspecting on earth! Indeed the devil as the Antichrist is coming down to you de jure, having tremendous influence to seduce spiritually, knowing that he has only a five-month reign. *{2 Co. 11:3-4; Mar. 13:17-19; 2 Ths. 2:7-12}*

The Dragon

On Earth

¹³And when the dragon saw that he was cast unto the earth, he persecuted the woman which brought forth the man child.

And when the serpent Satan perceived that he was cast down into the earth to the state of degradation, he earnestly pursued to persecute mother Israel who brought forth Christ the Messiah in the flesh.

Christ Yasha`yah's lineage and heritage is of Israel, from the king line tribes of Judah and the priesthood tribe of Levi. He is Melchizedek, the King of righteousness, and the High Priest of Israel and the gentile nations. *{Gen. 3:14-15, 14:18-20; Isa. 7:14; Rev. 12:6}*

¹⁴And to the woman were given two wings of a great eagle, that she might fly into the wilderness into her place, where she is nourished for a time, and times, and half a time, from the face of the serpent.

And to the twelve tribes of Israel (and the elect servants of

God) were given the gospel armor of Almighty God YHVH (as the protective veil), that they might protect themselves among the gentile nations, in His wisdom and knowledge, where they are nourished with the truth and understanding of His Word during the five-month reign of the seducer Antichrist.

The wings symbolize God YHVH as our Great Eagle and fortress, which His children take refuge under. A time, times, and half a time is three-and-a-half years; this is the hour of temptation which was reduced to a five-month period. *{Isa. 11:16, 43:1-15; Rev. 3:10; Mar. 13:20-22; Eze. 20:33-38; Deu. 4:6-9; 32:10-12; Mal. 4:2}*

¹⁵And the serpent cast out of his mouth water as a flood after the woman, that he might cause her to be carried away of the flood.

And the old serpent Satan spewed out of his mouth a flood of lies and deception after the elect servants of God, in an attempt to spiritually seduce them with strong delusion.

The truth and wisdom of God's Word swallows up lies and deception; therefore, be in the ark of the covenant, God's Word in truth with understanding, and not drowning and carried away by Satan's flood of lies and deception. *{Ex. 7:8-13; Isa. 59:19}*

¹⁶And the earth helped the woman, and the earth opened her mouth, and swallowed up the flood which the dragon cast out of his mouth.

And the earth helped the elect, and utilized the law of nature to swallow up death and the flood of lies which spewed from the mouth of the serpent Satan. *{Gen. 9:12-16; Exo. 14:21-31, 15:9-13; Isa.*

43:1-6, 59:16-21; Num. 16:28-35; Rom. 2:14-15; 1 Co. 15:54-55}

¹⁷And the dragon was wroth with the woman, and went to make war with the remnant of her seed, which keep the commandments of God, and have the testimony of Jesus Christ.

And the serpent Satan became enraged with mother Eve, and went away to make war with the remnant of her promised seed, Israel and God's elect servants, who know and obey the commandments of God YHVH in truth, and understand the eternal saving purpose of Christ Yasha`yah.

If you are a true believer in Christ and have the seal of God in your mind, then you are also a remnant of her seed through Abraham. {Gen. 3:13-15, 17:5-9; Eze. 14:22-23; Rom. 4:16-17; Gal. 4:23-31; Rev. 7:9}

Chapter 13

The Image of the Two Beasts

On Earth

¹And I stood upon the sand of the sea, and saw a beast rise up out of the sea, having seven heads and ten horns, and upon his horns ten crowns, and upon his heads the name of blasphemy.

And I (John) stood above the multitude on earth, and witnessed Satan's one-world government ascending out of the multitude, possessing ten supernatural, fallen angels and the seven continents; and given to his supernatural, fallen angels was ten kingdoms, and upon his systems of operation the reputation of blasphemy.

This first image of the beast is political, as a one-world government. The prince of this world Satan, as the Antichrist, returns de facto to earth peacefully, prospering everyone, claiming to bring about one-world peace. The seven heads represent the seven continents and the nations' system of operation, in which Satan has dominion by manipulating the four hidden dynasties (the beast system). {Dan. 8:23-25; Isa. 14:12; Zec. 8:23; Rev. 17:15}

²And the beast which I saw was like unto a leopard, and his feet were as the feet of a bear, and his mouth as the mouth of a lion: and the dragon gave him his power, and his seat, and great authority.

And the one-world government that I witnessed was swift and corrupt, and put its foot to vanquish, and its influence was ferocious with destructive leadership: and the serpent Satan empowered the one-world government, and established its sovereignty and great authority.

The beast system (being the four hidden dynasties) is compared to a leopard because of its spots and blemishes, which represent the imperfection and corruptness of the system. Its source will not be recognized by the people at the outset. *{2 Ths. 2:3-11; Isa. 14:12-14; Mar. 13:14-15; Jer. 5:6-7; Dan. 7:4-8, 19-27, 11:21}*

> **³And I saw one of his heads as it were wounded to death; and his deadly wound was healed: and all the world wondered after the beast.**

And I witnessed the one-world government which was inoperative at the time; however, Satan, as the Antichrist, made it to become a reality: and all the unsuspecting and biblically illiterate people of the world marveled and followed after the one-world government (beast system).

Before Satan's return de facto as the Antichrist, the one-world government is only a concept. However, when he is loosed from the pit of the abyss, all the biblically illiterate people on earth will follow and support his illusion of world peace. *{Dan. 9:27; Mar. 13:14-30; 2 Ths. 2:3-10}*

> **⁴And they worshipped the dragon which gave power unto the beast: and they worshipped the beast, saying, Who is like unto the beast? Who is able to make war with him?**

And the biblically illiterate people worshiped the serpent Satan as the Antichrist, who had empowered the one-world government: and they worshiped the one-world government, saying, What is like this one-world government? And who is able to make war with it?

Satan as the Antichrist will come in peacefully, prospering everyone, ceasing wars, paying off debts, and performing miraculous acts. He will be acclaimed by the people on this account. Having control over the four hidden dynasties gives Satan dominion over the world. War cannot be made against a one-world government, since there would be no other government to stand and fight against it. *{Mar. 13:9-14; Dan. 8:23-25, 9:26-27, 11:21-24; Mat. 10:34}*

⁵And there was given unto him a mouth speaking great things and blasphemies; and power was given unto him to continue forty and two months.

And Satan, as the Antichrist, spewed from his mouth abominable lies and blasphemies in claiming to be the Christ of God; and authority was given to him to reign for five months.

Forty-two months is equal to the three-and-a-half-year period of the Antichrist's prophesied reign on earth, but was reduced by God to a five-month period. *{Mar. 13:20; 2 Ths. 2:1-12}*

⁶And he opened his mouth in blasphemy against God, to blaspheme His name, and His tabernacle, and them that dwell in heaven.

And he opened his mouth unto blasphemies against God, to blaspheme the Christ of God, and the many-membered body of Christ, and those tabernacling in heaven. *{Dan. 7:25, 11:36-37}*

⁷And it was given unto him to make war with the saints, and to overcome them: and power was given him over all kindreds, and tongues, and nations.

And he was given the consent to wage war against God's elect servants, and to deliver them up to his councils (for a testimony against him): and authority was given to him over every biblically illiterate tribe, people, language, and nation. *{Rev. 2:10; Mar. 13:9-13; Dan. 7:21-22, 8:12, 24, 11:31-35; Isa. 10:16-25}*

⁸And all that dwell upon the earth shall worship him, whose names are not written in the Book of Life of the Lamb slain from the foundation of the world.

And all of the biblically illiterate people dwelling on the earth will worship the Antichrist, everyone whose name has not been written in the Book of Life of the Lamb Christ before the foundation of this second earth age. *{Rev. 17:8}*

⁹If any man has an ear, let him hear.

If any man will listen, let him hear with understanding. *{Hos. 14:9; Jn. 5:39}*

¹⁰He that leadeth into captivity shall go into captivity: he that killeth with the sword must be killed with the sword. Here is the patience and the faith of the saints.

If anyone is for the captivity of Christ (good), or Satan (evil), into that captivity he will go: if anyone will kill with the sword of Satan's lies and deceptions, it behooves him to be killed by the exacting retribution of Christ's truth and righteousness. This is the endurance and the faith of God's elect servants.

This verse is a Hebrew idiom for destiny. The message expresses that one reaps what one sows. The patience and the faith of God's elect are to know that their righteous deeds and morals will be justly rewarded, and the evil deeds of their enemies will also be justly rewarded. {Pro. 26:27; Ecc. 12:13-14; Gal. 6:7-9; Jer. 15:2-3; Mat. 26:52}

¹¹And I beheld another beast coming up out of the earth; and he had two horns like a lamb, and he spake as a dragon.

And I witnessed another beast, the Antichrist, arise out of the inhabitants on earth; and he had miraculous powers, and resembled the Lamb Christ Yasha`yah, but he spoke lies as the serpent Satan.

This beast is distinguished from that of verse one: the beast of verse one is political, while this beast is religious. The figurative of the *beast* is depicted as the Antichrist, both his person and his kingdom and power. {Rev. 6:2; Zec. 11:15-17; 2 Co. 11:13-15; Dan. 7:20-21}

¹²And he exerciseth all the power of the first beast before him, and causeth the earth and them which dwell therein to worship the first beast, whose deadly wound was healed.

And the Antichrist executed total authority over the one-world government, and caused the biblically illiterate people of the world to worship the beast system, bringing one-worldism to a reality. {Dan. 8:24-25, 11:21-35; Nah. 3:19}

¹³And he doeth great wonders, so that he maketh fire come down from heaven on the earth in the sight of men,

And he performed great miracles, such as causing lightning to strike on the earth in the presence of the people,

Miracles of themselves are no proof of a Divine mission. Our Heavenly Father's miracles are signs for His servants to meditate upon, but the miracles of the Antichrist are used to impress credulous unbelievers. *{Mat. 24:24; Mar. 13:22}*

¹⁴And deceiveth them that dwell on the earth by the means of those miracles which he had power to do in the sight of the beast; saying to them that dwell on the earth, that they should make an image to the beast, which had the wound by a sword, and did live.

And he deceived the unsuspecting and biblically illiterate people by way of those miracles that were given to him to perform while manipulating the one-world government; telling the people dwelling on earth that they should make a religion of one-worldism, which was condemned by the elect servants witnessing the truth of God, but did exist because of credulous unbelievers. *{Dan. 9:26-27; 2 Ths. 2:9-12; 1 Tim. 4:1-3}*

¹⁵And he had power to give life unto the image of the beast, that the image of the beast should both speak, and cause that as many as would not worship the image of the beast should be killed.

And power was given to the Antichrist to give operation to the religion of the one-world government, so that the religion of the one-world government would both function, and cause all who would not give obeisance to be excommunicated from society. *{Dan. 2:31-38, 4:17}*

¹⁶And he causeth all, both small and great, rich and poor, free and bond, to receive a mark in their right hand, or in their foreheads:

And he caused all the unsuspecting and biblically illiterate people, regardless of their status in life, to participate in his evil works, and receive his seal of deception in their minds: {Eze. 3:8-11}

¹⁷And that no man might buy or sell, save he that had the mark, or the name of the beast, or the number of his name.

And that no one could buy or sell, except those having Satan's seal of deception, believing in his one-world government, and worshiping him as the Antichrist.

During this time, if a person does not participate in or support the one-world government along with the rest of the deceived world, they will be classified in society as a rebel and evildoer. In actuality, the unsuspecting and biblically illiterate ones in their ignorance are the evildoers. {Zec. 8:9-10}

¹⁸Here is wisdom. Let him that hath understanding count the number of the beast: for it is the number of a man; and his number is Six hundred threescore and six.

Herein is wisdom. Let the person who has understanding count the number that depicts the Antichrist: for it is the number of the man Satan; and his number is 666.

The Greek word for "count" is *psephizo* (5585), which means "to use pebbles in enumeration." This word is derived from *psephos*

(5586), meaning "a pebble as worn smooth by handling." The people of the world are to take into account the evil deeds of Satan since the Garden of Eden. In a spiritual sense, the counting pebble is worn smooth from counting Satan's innumerable wicked works. Also, take note that the Greek word for "666" is *chi xi stigma* (5516), and the word *stigma* (4742) means "a mark for recognition of ownership," also known as the "mark of the beast." When the number of the beast is analyzed, wisdom surely lies therein of who this man is.

The number "666" signifies the sixth seal, trumpet, and vial. This verse is a warning to all, that Satan's reign as the Antichrist takes place during the sixth seal, trumpet, and vial. Those who do not take heed to this warning are and will be deceived, believing that Christ has come to rapture them away, and not understanding that Satan appears first as the Antichrist to deceive all who are biblically illiterate. The true Savior, Christ Yasha`yah, does not return to earth until the seventh seal, trumpet, and vial.

Numbered references are derived from the *Strong's Exhaustive Concordance with Greek and Hebrew Dictionary*. {Isa. 14:16-17, 57:6; Jn. 8:41-47; Mat. 13:37-40; Deu. 32:29-34; Gen. 4:15}

Chapter 14

The Harvest of the World

In Heaven

¹And I looked, and, lo, a Lamb stood on the Mount Zion, and with Him an hundred forty and four thousand, having His Father's name written in their foreheads.

And I (John) witnessed the true Messiah Christ Yasha`yah standing on Mount Zion along with 144,000 from the tribes of Israel, having the seal of Christ and God YHVH in their minds.

The 144,000 is the second elect group mentioned in Revelation 7:4. *{Isa. 2:3-4, 52:6-8; Rev. 7:3-8; Heb. 12:22-23}*

²And I heard a voice from heaven, as the voice of many waters, and as the voice of a great thunder: and I heard the voice of harpers harping with their harps:

And I heard from heaven the voice of many people, and the rumbling voices of Elohim (God): and I heard the sound of harpists playing on their harps: *{Ex. 9:28; Job 38:7}*

³And they sung as it were a new song before the throne, and before the four beasts, and the elders: and no man could learn that song but the hundred and forty and four thousand, which were redeemed from the earth.

And they sang as it were a new song before the throne of God, and before the four living creature guards, and the twenty-four elders: and no one was able to learn the song except the 144,000, having been purchased from the earth. *{Rev. 5:9-14}*

⁴*These are they which were not defiled with women; for they are virgins. These are they which follow the Lamb whithersoever he goeth. These were redeemed from among men, being the first fruits unto God and to the Lamb.*

These elect are the ones who have not been seduced by the great harlot Satan as the Antichrist; for they are pure indeed (with the seal of God's truth in their minds). These are the ones who accompany Christ Yasha`yah in the truth. These have been purchased from among men as being sacred and dear beyond all others to God and Christ. *{Rom. 8:23-39; 2 Co. 11:2-4; Mat. 20:16; Mar. 13:17; Jn. 17:12-26; Rev. 20:4}*

⁵*And in their mouth was found no guile: for they are without fault before the throne of God.*

And in their mouth was found no deceit: for they are spiritually blameless before the throne of God YHVH. *{Eph. 1:3-5}*

Chapter 14: The Harvest of the World

The Fifth Vision

On Earth

⁶And I saw another angel fly in the midst of heaven, having the everlasting gospel to preach unto them that dwell on the earth, and to every nation, and kindred, and tongue, and people;

And I (John) witnessed another angel flying in mid-heaven, preaching the eternal saving purpose (glad tidings) of God and Christ to all mortal souls dwelling on the earth;

Once Satan's reign on earth as the Antichrist ends, we enter into the Day of the Lord, the millennium period. The mortal souls represent those seduced and liable to be blotted out forever. During the millennium, the mortal souls will be sternly taught discipline by God's elect servants for a one-thousand-year period on earth without any of Satan's influence. After the millennium period, the great white throne judgment of God YHVH occurs. {Mar. 13:10, 31; Rev. 20:1-3; Eze. 44:23-25}

⁷Saying with a loud voice, Fear God, and give glory to Him; for the hour of His judgment is come: and worship Him that made heaven, and earth, and the sea, and the foundations of waters.

Saying with a mighty voice, Reverence and fear God YHVH, and give Him glory; because the time of His righteous judgment is executed: and worship Him that created heaven, earth, and everything therein.

The Day of Judgment is great reward for God's elect and those overcoming, but for the mortal souls who are seduced by the harlot Satan it is damnation. *{Mat. 10:28; Jer. 9:23-24; Ex. 20:1-6; Isa. 61:1-2; Luk. 4:18-19; 2 Ths. 9:12}*

⁸And there followed another angel, saying, Babylon is fallen, is fallen, that great city, because she made all nations drink of the wine of the wrath of her fornication.

And a second angel followed, saying, Babel has been overthrown, that state of great confusion (the four hidden dynasties), because the harlot Satan broke all the biblically illiterate people of the world in pieces with the love-potion (false truths) of her immorality.

Babylon was known as the "gate of gods," and also means "confusion;" because religion is babel and confusion, but Christianity is the reality of God and Christ. *{Isa. 14:15-17, 21:9, 27:1; Jer. 51:6-9; Psa. 73:27; Pro. 7:1-27}*

⁹And the third angel followed them, saying with a loud voice, If any man worship the beast and his image, and receive his mark in his forehead, or in his hand,

And a third angel followed, saying with a mighty voice, If anyone worships the spurious messiah Antichrist and his religious system, receiving his seal of deception in their mind, or participating in his evil works, *{Dan. 11:21-24}*

¹⁰The same shall drink of the wine of the wrath of God, which is poured out without mixture into the cup of His indignation; and he shall be tormented with fire and brimstone in the presence of the holy angels, and

in the presence of the Lamb:

The same will also be broken in pieces with the indignation of God's fiery wine, which is poured out undiluted to those whom He is about to punish in their own folly and madness; and they will be tormented with burning shame and humiliation in the presence of the heavenly hosts, and the Lamb Christ Yasha`yah: *{Isa. 51:17-23; Luk. 16:22-29}*

[11] And the smoke of their torment ascendeth up forever and ever: and they had no rest day nor night, who worship the beast and his image, and whosoever receiveth the mark of his name.

And the smoke of their strong delusion, by which they were tormented, ascended forever: and they had no rest or peace, whosoever worshiped Satan as the Antichrist and his religious system, receiving his seal of deception in their minds.

The mortal souls who do not overcome Satan as the Antichrist are condemned to make way for a holy and perfect heaven on earth. God's saints that overcome receive true rest and peace of their souls and eternal life in Christ. But those that do not overcome are blotted out forever at the great white throne judgment of God YHVH, with no chance to receive Christ our Sabbath (Rest) ever again. *{Psa. 37:18-20, 34; 2 Pet. 3:10; Dan. 9:22-27; Heb. 3:7-11, 18-19, 4:1-11; Isa. 34:8-10}*

[12] Here is the patience of the saints: here are they that keep the commandments of God, and the faith of Jesus.

Herein is the endurance of God's election: they hold firm the commandments of God YHVH in truth and the faith which Christ Yasha`yah gives. *{Mat. 24:40-41; Jn. 16:33}*

¹³ And I heard a voice from heaven saying unto me, Write, Blessed are the dead which die in the Lord from henceforth: Yea, saith the Spirit, that they may rest from their labours; and their works do follow them.

And I (John) heard a voice out of heaven saying, Write, Happy are they which die believing in Christ Yasha`yah from henceforth: Surely, said the Holy Spirit, for they will rest from all of their toilsome labors; and their works do follow with them to heaven. *{1 Ths. 4:13-18; Heb. 4:8-11; 2 Co. 3:17}*

¹⁴ And I looked, and behold a white cloud, and upon the cloud, One sat like unto the Son of Man, having on His head a golden crown, and in His hand a sharp sickle.

And I looked and witnessed a glorious throne, and on the throne sitting was Christ Yasha`yah, adorned with His crown of glory, and in His hand was a sharp sickle (for harvesting).

It is harvest time spiritually for Christ our Lord to reap, separating the wheat, signifying God's elect, from the tares, signifying Satan's children (the Kenites) and his followers. *{Mat. 13:37-43}*

¹⁵ And another angel came out of the temple, crying with a loud voice to Him that sat on the cloud, Thrust in Thy sickle, and reap: for the time is come for Thee to reap; for the harvest of the earth is ripe.

And a fourth angel came out of the Temple of God, shouting with a mighty voice to Christ Yasha`yah, saying, Put forth Your sickle, and reap: because the time has come to reap; for the harvest of this second earth age is ready for judgment. *{Joe. 3:13}*

¹⁶ And He that sat on the cloud thrust in His sickle on the earth; and the earth was reaped.

And Christ Yasha`yah put forth His sharp sickle upon the earth; and the people were harvested for judgment. *{Isa. 2:3-4}*

¹⁷ And another angel came out of the Temple, which is in heaven, he also having a sharp sickle.

And a fifth angel came out of the heavenly Temple, also having a sharp sickle.

¹⁸ And another angel came out from the altar, which had power over fire; and cried with a loud cry to him that had the sharp sickle, saying, Thrust in thy sharp sickle, and gather the clusters of the vine of the earth; for her grapes are fully ripe.

And a sixth angel came out from the altar, having authority over the altar fire; and He shouted with a mighty voice to the angel with the sharp sickle, saying, Put forth your sharp sickle, and harvest all of the mortal souls; for they are ready for judgment.

The deceived souls of the world are represented in this verse as overripe grapes on a vine. A sickle is utilized for harvesting grain, not vines of grapes. This signifies a great deal of thrashing and bloodshed taking place spiritually for the people who are found deceived and unlearned concerning God's will and plan of salvation. *{Mat. 13:39-43; Isa. 34:1-8, 63:1-6; Joe. 3:12-16}*

¹⁹And the angel thrust in his sickle into the earth, and gathered the vine of the earth, and cast it into the great winepress of the wrath of God.

And the angel put forth his sharp sickle upon the earth, and harvested the mortal souls, and cast them into the great thrashing of the indignation of God. *{Am. 8:2-3}*

²⁰And the winepress was trodden without the city, and blood came out of the winepress, even unto the horse bridles, by the space of a thousand and six hundred furlongs.

And the thrashing was carried throughout the city, and blood flowed out from the thrashing, as high as the horses' bridles, for a distance of 200 miles.

A thousand and six hundred furlongs is about 200 miles, indicating the immense number of deceived people that will receive destruction. During this time, God's indignation on the mortal souls is torment; but at the end of the millennium, the damnation is the perishing of their souls in the lake of fire forever. *{Deu. 32:32-35, 42-43; Isa. 63:2-3; Luk. 19:26-27; Rev. 11:1-2, 20:14-15; Jer. 25:15-38}*

Chapter 15

THE SEVEN ANGELS WITH THE SEVEN LAST PLAGUES

In Heaven

¹And I saw another sign in heaven, great and marvelous, seven angels having the seven last plagues; for in them is filled up the wrath of God.

And I (John) witnessed in heaven another great and marvelous sign, seven angel of God having the seven final plagues; because in them is the full measure of God's indignation.

²And I saw as it were a sea of glass mingled with fire: and them that had gotten the victory over the beast, and over his image, and over his mark, and over the number of his name, stand on the sea of glass, having the harps of God.

And I saw the holy of holies, along with the Shekhinah Glory of God YHVH: and the elect of God who overcame the Antichrist, his religious system, his seal of deception, and the number 666 of the man Satan, standing in the holy of holies, having the harps of God (to which the praises of God are sung in heaven). *{Heb. 9:1-28}*

³And they sing the song of Moses the servant of God,

and the song of the Lamb, saying, Great and marvelous are Thy works, LORD God Almighty; just and true are Thy ways, Thou King of saints.

And they sang the song of God's servant Moses, and the song of the Lord Yasha`yah, saying, Great and marvelous are Your works, YHVH God Almighty; Righteous and true are Your ways, King of the nations! *{Deu. 31:30, 32:1-43; Ex. 15:1-19; Psa. 86:9-12; Isa. 66:15-23}*

[4]Who shall not fear Thee, O LORD, and glorify Thy name? For Thou only art holy: for all nations shall come and worship before Thee, for Thy judgments are made manifest.

Who will not reverence and fear You, YHVH, and glorify Your name? For You only are holy: for every knee shall bow and worship before You, because Your righteous acts have been revealed. *{Phn. 2:9-11}*

[5]And after that I looked, and behold, the Temple of the tabernacle of the testimony in heaven was opened:

Afterward I looked, and saw the Temple of the Ark of the Covenant as it was opened in heaven: *{Deu. 31:25-26; Rev. 11:19}*

[6]And the seven angels came out of the Temple, having the seven plagues, clothed in pure and white linen, and having their breasts girded with golden girdles.

And the seven angels came forth out of the heavenly Temple, having the seven plagues of God's indignation, clothed in linen with precious stones pure and bright, and their chests girded about with the gospel armor. *{Eph. 6:13-17}*

⁷And one of the four beasts gave unto the seven angels seven golden vials full of the wrath of God, who liveth forever and ever.

And one of the four living creatures gave to the seven angels, seven broad, shallow cups filled with the indignation of God, Who is Eternal. *{Isa. 51:22-23; Mat. 26:39-42}*

⁸And the Temple was filled with smoke from the glory of God, and from His power; and no man was able to enter into the temple, till the seven plagues of the seven angels were fulfilled.

And the heavenly Temple was closed off from the glory and miraculous power of God; and no one was allowed to enter the Temple until the seven plagues of God's fierce indignation were executed.

God will not allow any soul into His holy presence and Temple that has not been properly tested and proven. *{Rev. 9:6}*

CHAPTER 16

THE SEVEN VIALS OF WRATH

On Earth

¹And I heard a great voice out of the Temple saying to the seven angels, Go your ways, and pour out the vials of the wrath of God upon the earth.

And I (John) heard a mighty voice out of the Temple saying to the seven angels of God, Go forth, and pour out the broad, shallow cups of God's indignation into the earth.

The plagues of God's wrath take place at the sixth trumpet during the reign of Satan as the Antichrist on Mount Zion in Jerusalem. *{2 Ths. 2:7-12; Nah. 1:2-3}*

²And the first went, and poured out his vial upon the earth; and there fell a noisome and grievous sore upon the men which had the mark of the beast, and upon them which worshipped his image.

And the first angel went forth, and poured out his broad, shallow cup into the earth; and there became a grievous and festering sore upon those who had the seal of the Antichrist's deception in their minds, and upon those worshiping his religious system. *{Mat. 24:48-51}*

³And the second angel poured out his vial upon the sea;

and it became as the blood of a dead man: and every living soul died in the sea.

And the second angel poured out his broad, shallow cup of strong delusion into the sea of biblically illiterate and unsuspecting people of the world; and they became as the spirit of a dead man: and every deceived, mortal soul died spiritually.

As in Revelation 8:8, these people are those who listen and follow after Satan, the prince of this world age, and his ways. They have no interest in researching the facts, or studying diligently to know God and Christ, or understanding His eternal saving purpose (gospel) in truth, chapter by chapter and verse by verse. *{Eze. 6:8-14; Rom. 11:4-8; 2 Ths. 2:9-12; Isa. 29:10-14, 54:1; Rev. 8:8, 11:6, 17:15}*

⁴And the third angel poured out his vial upon the rivers and fountains of waters; and they became blood.

And the third angel poured out his broad, shallow cup of strong delusion onto the supposed preachers and people of the Christian communities; and they became spiritually dead. *{Eze. 31:4-5; Rev. 8:10; 1 Co. 3:12-17}*

⁵And I heard the angel of the waters say, Thou art righteous, O Lord, Which art, and wast, and shalt be, because Thou hast judged thus.

And I heard Michael, the angel of the people, say, Righteous are You, Thee Holy One, Who is the same yesterday, today, and forever, because You have judged rightly. *{Heb. 13:8, Dan. 12:1}*

⁶For they have shed the blood of saints and prophets,

and Thou hast given them blood to drink; for they are worthy.

For the offspring of Satan, the Kenites, and their sea of followers, have murdered God's elect and prophets of old, and You have given them the cup of vengeance to drink; for they are deserving of it. *{Isa. 51:17-23; Luk. 11:46-54; Mat. 23:29-36, 26:39; Jn. 8:42-47}*

⁷*And I heard another out of the altar say, Even so, LORD God Almighty, true and righteous are Thy judgments.*

And I heard the angel Gabriel out of the altar of God, say, Yes, YHVH God Almighty, true and righteous are Your divine judgments. *{Luk. 1:19; Rev. 6:9-11}*

⁸*And the fourth angel poured out his vial upon the sun; and power was given unto him to scorch men with fire.*

And the fourth angel poured out his broad, shallow cup of the fire of God; and it was given to God's elect and two anointed witnesses to torture the unsuspecting and biblically illiterate people with the truth and Holy Spirit.

The sun represents the children of light and of the day, having the Holy Spirit. The fire represents God as the consuming fire and His Holy Spirit, which scorches evildoers, but enlightens and purifies the true believers so that they can share more and more in His likeness. *{2 Kgs. 1:10-14; Joe. 2:11, 3:28-32; Mar. 13:9-11; 1 Ths. 5:5; Rev. 11:3-6}*

⁹*And men were scorched with great heat, and blasphemed the name of God, which hath power over these plagues:*

and they repented not to give Him glory.

And they were tortured with the truth and Holy Spirit of God, and blasphemed God YHVH, the One having the authority over these heavy afflictions: and they did not repent to give Him glory.

The deceived religious communities loved and honored God with their mouths, and truly thought they were doing His will, but were confused between the truth of Christ and the lies of the Antichrist. They believed that the one-verse, out of context, sweet-sounding sermons, half-truths, and traditions of men being taught by their preachers, were the will and plan of God's salvation. They never studied in depth, nor were taught in depth, to find out the real truth of the matter. *{Joe. 1:8-13; Isa. 29:10-15, 30:33; Hos. 11:7}*

¹⁰ And the fifth angel poured out his vial upon the seat of the beast; and his kingdom was full of darkness; and they gnawed their tongues for pain,

And the fifth angel poured out his broad, shallow cup on the throne of the Antichrist on Mount Zion in Jerusalem; and his sovereignty became full of strong delusion and wickedness; and the unsuspecting and biblically illiterate people were agonized from the distress, *{Mat. 24:15; 2 Ths. 2:3-4; Rev. 2:13, 9:2}*

¹¹ And blasphemed the God of heaven because of their pains and their sores, and repented not of their deeds.

And they cursed God YHVH on account of their distresses from their unbelief and elements of corruption, and refused to repent from their evil works. *{Isa. 10:1-7}*

Chapter 16: The Seven Vials of Wrath

¹²And the sixth angel poured out his vial upon the great river Euphrates; and the water thereof was dried up, that the way of the kings of the east might be prepared.

And the sixth angel poured out his broad, shallow cup on the great river Euphrates; and the water thereof was dried up spiritually, so that the path of the kings, which come with the false morning star Lucifer, might be prepared for the spiritual battle.

These kings are the ten supernatural, fallen angels that come to reign with the Antichrist during the hour of temptation. *The east* is an idiom for the rising of the sun, representing Satan as Lucifer, the false morning star. The river Euphrates separates the city of Babylon (confusion) from the city of Jerusalem (peace), and is also symbolic of the great gulf fixed in heaven that separates the pit of the abyss from Paradise. *{Rev. 9:14-15, 17:12, 16-17; Jer. 46:3-10, 50:25; Dan. 11:30-35}*

¹³And I saw three unclean spirits like frogs come out of the mouth of the dragon, and out of the mouth of the beast, and out of the mouth of the false prophet.

And I witnessed three impure spirits come out of the mouth of the serpent Satan, and out of the one-world government, and out of the spurious messiah Antichrist. *{1 Jn. 4:1-3; Ex. 8:2-14; Rev. 9:18-19, 13:11-17, 19:20}*

¹⁴For they are the spirits of devils, working miracles, which go forth unto the kings of the earth and of the whole world, to gather them to the battle of that great day of God Almighty.

For they are indeed the spirits of demons, performing

miraculous acts, which go forth to the biblically illiterate world rulers and all deceived people living on the inhabited earth, to draw them together to the spiritual battle of the great day of God, the Almighty. *{Mar. 13:21-23}*

¹⁵Behold, I come as a thief. Blessed is he that watcheth, and keepeth his garments, lest he walk naked, and they see his shame.

Behold, I (Christ) am coming when you least expect it. Blessed are they who are watching spiritually for the signs of the end times, keeping their gospel armor on and intact, so as to not walk unrighteous, and others see their indecent (lewd) acts. *{Luk. 12:37-40; 1 Ths. 5:2-10; Rev. 3:17-18}*

¹⁶And he gathered them together into a place called in the Hebrew tongue Armageddon.

And the Antichrist gathered all the deceived people together into a place which in Hebrew is called Har-Magedon.

Armageddon is the city of Megiddo, which means "the place of crowds." Megiddo was a city of the Manassites, situated in the great plain of the tribe of Issachar, and was famous for two great slaughters, one of the Canaanites, and the other of the Israelites. For the end times, this symbolizes the great slaughter of the enemies of God and Christ. Just as the city of Megiddo is a historically known battlefield, it is the battlefield of the Antichrist and his followers in the end times. In the Greek language, Armageddon is known as *Har-Megiddon*, meaning "hill country," representing Mount Carmel in Jerusalem. *{Mar. 13:14; Zec. 12:11; Jgs. 5:19; 2 Kgs. 23:26-30; 2 Chr. 35:20-23; 2 Ths. 2:4}*

¹⁷And the seventh angel poured out his vial into the air; and there came a great voice out of the Temple of heaven, from the throne, saying, It is done.

And the seventh angel poured out his broad, shallow cup into the atmosphere, and the people on earth became transformed into their spiritual, breath of life bodies; and there came a word of command out of the heavenly Temple from the throne of God, saying, It is finished. {1 Ths. 4:15-17; 2 Ths. 2:7-9; Zec. 14:12; 1 Co. 15:49-57}

¹⁸And there were voices, and thunders, and lightnings; and there was a great earthquake, such as was not since men were upon the earth, so mighty an earthquake, and so great.

And there were flashes of lightning, voices and the rumbling voices of Elohim (God); and there was a massive earthquake, such as was not since the beginning of the first earth age unto this time, so drastic was the earthquake.

This earthquake occurs when Christ Yasha`yah descends from heaven, and steps foot onto earth at the Mount of Olives as King of kings and Lord of lords. {Ex. 9:28; Jer. 4:22-28; Mar. 13:18-27; Heb. 12:25-29}

¹⁹And the great city was divided into three parts, and the cities of the nations fell: and great Babylon came in remembrance before God, to give unto her the cup of the wine of the fierceness of His wrath.

And the great city of Jerusalem became split into three parts, and the cities of the nations were destroyed: and Satan, the author of great confusion, was remembered in the eyes of God YHVH, to break the great harlot into pieces with the vengeance of His indignation. *{Isa. 51:17; Zec. 14:1-5; Mar. 13:1-4; Dan. 4:30-31}*

²⁰ And every island fled away, and the mountains were not found.

And every small country and nation's kingdom was done away with. *{Jer. 44:13}*

²¹ And there fell upon men a great hail out of heaven, every stone about the weight of a talent: and men blasphemed God because of the plague of the hail; for the plague thereof was exceeding great.

And there fell upon the deceived people great hailstones from heaven, each stone exceeding the weight of one hundred pounds: and they blasphemed God YHVH because of the affliction of the hail; for the affliction thereof was dreadful. *{Jos. 10:11; Isa. 30:27-28; Eze. 38:19-23; Luk. 12:45-49; Rev. 6:14-17}*

CHAPTER 17

THE END OF THE DOMINION OF SIN

On Earth

¹And there came one of the seven angels, which had the seven vials, and talked with me, saying unto me, Come hither; I will show unto thee the judgment of the great whore that sitteth upon many waters:

And one of the seven angels, having the seven broad, shallow cups of God's indignation, spoke with me (John), saying, Come here; I will show you the condemnation of the great harlot Satan, as the state of great confusion residing upon the masses: *{Am. 3:11; Eze. 28:16-19; Rev. 15:7; 1 Pet. 5:8}*

²With whom the kings of the earth have committed fornication, and the inhabitants of the earth have been made drunk with the wine of her fornication.

With whom the rulers of the world committed acts of idolatry, and they that inhabit the earth were broken in pieces with the love-potion (false truths) of her immorality. *{Isa. 14:16-18}*

³So he carried me away in the Spirit into the wilderness: and I saw a woman sit upon a scarlet coloured beast, full of names of blasphemy, having seven heads and ten horns.

And he carried me away in the Spirit into a wilderness (the last days on earth): and I witnessed the scarlet woman Satan (as the state of great confusion), regarded as typifying vice overlaid with gaudy pageantry, residing upon the spurious messiah Antichrist, being full of blasphemous names, and possessing the seven continents and the ten supernatural, fallen angels. {2 Ths. 2:7-9; Mar. 13:28-30; Jn. 12:31; Dan. 9:26-27, 11:21-24; Rev. 13:1}

⁴And the woman was arrayed in purple and scarlet colour, and decked with gold and precious stones and pearls, having a golden cup in her hand full of abominations and filthiness of her fornication:

And the harlot Satan as the state of great confusion (being the four hidden dynasties) was arrayed as the truth of God, and disguised as holy and righteous, working all power, signs, and lying wonders, being full of idolatry and the impurities of her immorality: {Pro. 6:23-29; Dan. 11:31-32; Jer. 51:6-10; 2 Co. 11:13-15; Deu. 13:1-5, 18:9-13}

⁵And upon her forehead was a name written, MYSTERY, BABYLON THE GREAT, THE MOTHER OF HARLOTS AND ABOMINATIONS OF THE EARTH.

And written on the forehead of the great harlot was the name MYSTERY OF INIQUITY, THE STATE OF GREAT CONFUSION, THE CREATOR AND HARBORER OF ALL IDOLATERS AND IDOLATRIES OF THE WORLD.

Mystery Babylon is the source of all confusion, idolatry, and systems of false worship. The mystery is an initiation into a new religion by secrecy: her new religion being apostasy. This is the mystery of iniquity that is identified in all the world's great religions. Instead of being devoted to the One and True God YHVH of the Bible, these religions substitute a god made with tangible materials, or simply from their imaginations; and their beliefs and worship consist of human merits and endeavors. *{Deu. 13:6; Luk. 21:34-35; Isa. 14:16-17; 2 Ths. 2:7-12; Rev. 17:18}*

⁶And I saw the woman drunken with the blood of the saints, and with the blood of the martyrs of Jesus: and when I saw her, I wondered with great admiration.

And I saw the religious harlot Satan drenched with the blood of the election, and with the blood of the two anointed witnesses of Christ Yasha`yah: and when I saw her, I marveled with great astonishment.

The election of God has been murdered throughout history by the followers of Satan's mysterious religious system, which seduced them into thinking that they were doing the will of God. The two anointed witnesses are murdered at the hand of Satan during his reign on earth as the Antichrist. *{Isa. 34:12-13; Mat. 23:29-37; Rev. 2:13, 6:9-11, 11:7-9}*

⁷And the angel said unto me, Wherefore didst thou marvel? I will tell thee the mystery of the woman, and of the beast that carrieth her, which hath the seven heads and ten horns.

And the angel said to me, Why are you astonished? I will reveal to you the mystery of the harlot Satan, even the Antichrist, whose coming is according to the working (energy) of Satan (in every power, sign and miraculous wonder of falsehood), who possesses the seven continents and the ten supernatural, fallen angels. *{2 Ths. 2:7-10}*

> ⁸*The beast that thou sawest was, and is not; and shall ascend out of the bottomless pit, and go into perdition: and they that dwell on the earth shall wonder, whose names were not written in the book of life from the foundation of the world, when they behold the beast that was, and is not, and yet is.*

The beast Satan that you witnessed was here in the first earth age and in the Garden of Eden as the serpent, and is currently detained in the pit of the abyss; and will ascend out of the abyss to reign as the Antichrist, and will go into perdition: and those dwelling on the earth will marvel, whose names have not been written in the Lamb's book of eternal life since the beginning of this second earth age, when they witness Satan, who was here in the first earth age, now imprisoned in the abyss, and yet will be on earth de facto as the Antichrist. *{Dan. 8:23-25; Isa. 14:14-18; Eze. 28:12-19; 1 Jn. 4:3}*

> ⁹*And here is the mind which hath wisdom. The seven heads are seven mountains, on which the woman sitteth.*

And here is the understanding of those with God's wisdom. The seven heads represent the seven continents, in which that state of great confusion resides.

> ¹⁰*And there are seven kings: five are fallen, and one is, and the other is not yet come; and when he cometh, he must continue a short space.*

Chapter 17: The End of the Dominion of Sin

And there are seven kingdoms in Jerusalem held by Satan: (1) Nebuchadrezzar, King of Babylon; (2) Medo-Persia; (3) Greece; (4) Rome (Christ's time period); (5) Mohammedans/Arabians, from 636 A.D. to 1948; (6) European Jews (the generation of the bad figs when the State of Israel was established in 1948 by the United Nations); and (7) Satan's reign as the Antichrist. Five of the kingdoms have fallen, the sixth will fall, and the seventh is forth coming; and when the Antichrist comes, he will reign de facto in Jerusalem for a five-month period. *{Jer. 24; 2 Ths. 2:3-9; Dan. 2:36-46, 5:18-20, 7:16-18, 8:20-25, 11:21-24; Mar. 13:28-30; Rev. 2:9}*

[11] And the beast that was, and is not, even he is the eighth, and is of the seven, and goeth into perdition.

And the beast Satan who was here in the first earth age and the Garden of Eden, and is currently detained and not on earth de facto, even he himself is the eighth, and is of the seven kingdoms, and will go into perdition.

The eighth beast represents Satan as the warlord when he is released from the bottomless pit the second time, returning to Jerusalem after the millennium, attempting to seduce and gather the mortal souls to battle again, even after being sternly taught discipline by God's elect servants. This is the final test before the great white throne judgment of God and the blotting out of the mortal souls. *{Rev. 20:6-10; Eze. 28:13-19}*

[12] And the ten horns, which thou sawest are ten kings, which have received no kingdom as yet; but receive power as kings one hour with the beast.

And the ten horns that you witnessed are the ten supernatural, fallen angels, which have not yet received their kingdom; but will be given authority as kings for a five-month period, along with Satan as the Antichrist. *{Dan. 7:7-8; Zec. 8:19-23; Rev. 12:9}*

> **¹³These have one mind, and shall give their power and strength unto the beast.**

These ten supernatural, fallen angels are of one mind, and they willingly give up their power and authority to the beast Satan as the Antichrist. *{Dan. 5:18-21}*

> **¹⁴These shall make war with the Lamb, and the Lamb shall overcome them: for He is Lord of lords, and King of kings: and they that are with Him are called, and chosen, and faithful.**

These and the Antichrist will make war against Christ Yasha`yah, and Christ Yasha`yah will prevail over them: because He is the Lord of lords, and King of kings: and those that are with Him are the called, and elect, and faithful ones. *{Rom. 8:26-33, 11:4-5; Mat. 20:16}*

> **¹⁵And he saith unto me, The waters which thou sawest, where the whore sitteth, are peoples, and multitudes, and nations, and tongues.**

And the angel said to me, The waters that you witnessed, where the state of great confusion resides, are the inhabitants and languages of the world. *{2 Co. 4:3-4}*

> **¹⁶And the ten horns which thou sawest upon the beast, these shall hate the whore, and shall make her desolate and naked, and shall eat her flesh, and burn her with fire.**

And the ten supernatural, fallen angels that you witnessed following the Antichrist, these will detest the harlot Satan, and will make her to be laid waste and exposed, and will devour and utterly consume her with lies and dishonor.

The ten fallen angels detest the harlot Satan because of his great deception and wickedness that leads them to perdition. *{Jer. 50:32; Dan. 11:26-29; Isa. 14:9-11}*

¹⁷For God hath put in their hearts to fulfill his will, and to agree, and give their kingdom unto the beast, until the Words of God shall be fulfilled.

For God YHVH has placed in their minds to execute His will, and to act in one mind, and to surrender their kingdom to the Antichrist, until the will and plan of God is fulfilled.

¹⁸And the woman which thou sawest is that great city, which reigneth over the kings of the earth.

And the harlot Satan that you witnessed is that great state of confusion (babel or Babylon), having sovereignty over the rulers of the world. *{Dan. 5:18-21, 8:22-25}*

Chapter 18

The Fall of Babylon

On Earth

¹And after these things I saw another angel come down from heaven, having great power; and the earth was lightened with His glory,

And after these things I (John) witnessed the Angel of the Lord descending out of heaven, invested with great authority; and the earth was illuminated with His Shekhinah glory, {Isa. 11:9-10; Heb. 2:14}

²And He cried mightily with a strong voice, saying, Babylon the great is fallen, is fallen, and is become the habitation of devils, and the hold of every foul spirit, and a cage of every unclean and hateful bird.

And He shouted with a mighty voice, saying, The state of great confusion is fallen under condemnation, and has become a dwelling place of demons, and a prison of every evil spirit being, and a prison of every creature unclean in thought and life that is hated. {Eze. 27:27,34; 1 Sam. 15:22-23; 1 Jn. 4:1-3; Isa. 21:9-10, 34:11-16, 61:1-2; Mat. 24:1-2; Jer. 51:6-8}

³For all nations have drunk of the wine of the wrath of her fornication, and the kings of the earth have committed fornication with her, and the merchants of the earth are waxed rich through the abundance of her delicacies.

For all nations have been broken in pieces with the love-potion (false truths) of the harlot Satan's immorality, and the rulers of the world have committed acts of idolatry with her four hidden dynasties (as the state of great confusion), and the merchants (including the perverse ministers and the Kenites) inhabiting the earth became enriched by the power of her wantonness.

The perverse and lawless preachers, teachers, and Kenites sinned habitually, selling lying publications, false prosperity messages, and ideologies of men to the unsuspecting and biblically illiterate people in exchange for their tithes and offerings. Wealth gained by the teachings of false doctrines, theories, and traditions of men, is ill-gotten gain. The harlot Satan, as the lawless one, rewards greatly those who execute his evil works and indulgences, having them to believe that God and Christ are blessing them. *{1 Tim. 6:3-6; Eze. 27:33; Isa. 29:10-14, 47:1-15; Tit. 1:10-12; Dan. 11:23-24; Jer. 50:25-38, 51:7-12; Pro. 21:6}*

⁴And I heard another voice from heaven, saying, Come out of her, My people, that ye be not partakers of her sins, and that ye receive not of her plagues.

And I heard the Lord's voice from heaven, saying, Come out of the state of confusion, My children (by knowing the eternal saving purpose of God and Christ), so that you have no fellowship in her sinful deeds, and that you receive not her afflictions.

One is delivered from the state of confusion by studying and researching diligently to know and understand God's Word in truth, being a chaste virgin spiritually for God and Christ. The plagues mentioned are the curses and afflictions which God sends upon the disobedient and biblically illiterate people of the world. *{Deu. 11:26-28, 28:15-68; Mar. 13:16-17; Isa. 10:20-24, 33:6; Jer. 50:4-9, 45-47; 2 Pet. 3:10}*

⁵*For her sins have reached unto heaven, and God hath remembered her iniquities.*

For the harlot Satan's sins have accumulated up to heaven, and God YHVH has kept record of her iniquities. *{Jer. 51:9; Isa. 14:13-15; Eze. 28:17-19; Rev. 13:6}*

⁶*Reward her even as she rewarded you, and double unto her double according to her works: in the cup which she hath filled fill to her double.*

Render to the harlot Satan as she has rendered, and fully compensate twofold according to her evil works: the fate which she has mingled, mingle to her double.

This is a Hebraism meaning "to undergo the same calamities which I undergo" (i.e. that he might be treated as harshly as I was), and is used of divine penalties. For each evil deed that Satan generates, God's elect servants answer with a double dose of God's truth and righteous indignation. *{2 Co. 10:3-6; Jer. 50:14-15, 51:24; Eph. 6:11-17; Deu. 19:19}*

⁷*How much she hath glorified herself, and lived deliciously, so much torment and sorrow give her: for she saith in her heart, I sit a queen, and am no widow, and shall see no sorrow.*

To the degree that the harlots of Satan glorified themselves and lived in self-indulgent luxury, to the same the degree give them torment and grief: because in their minds they boast, I reign as queen (of money-changers), and are one in spirit with my king the Antichrist, and will never see mourning. *{Zep. 2:15; Dan. 8:24-25; Isa. 47:8-15; Mat. 7:21-23}*

⁸Therefore shall her plagues come in one day, death, and mourning, and famine; and she shall be utterly burned with fire: for strong is the LORD God Who judgeth her.

For this cause, in the Day of the Lord their afflictions will come, pestilence, mourning and famine (for hearing the truth of God's Word); and the state of great confusion will be completely consumed by the Holy Spirit of God: for omnipotent is God YHVH Who condemns her. *{Mat. 5:19-20; Jas. 2:12-13; Heb. 12:29; Isa. 13:19-20; Dan. 8:24-25 Jer. 50:13, 39-40}*

⁹And kings of the earth, who have committed fornication and lived deliciously with her, shall bewail her, and lament for her, when they shall see the smoke of her burning,

And the rulers of the world, who have committed acts of idolatry and lived in self-indulgent luxury with the state of great confusion, will mourn in devastation over her four hidden dynasties, when they witness the smoke of her destruction,

These *kings of the earth* are those of Revelation 17:2 and 17:18. They are always seen in connection with Babylon (the state of confusion) or the beast system (the four hidden dynasties), as opposed to the *ten supernatural kings* of 17:3, 7, 12, and 16, which are never seen by John separately from the beast Antichrist. *{Eze. 26:15-21, 27:32-36; Jas. 5:5; 1 Pet. 4:12-13; Isa. 14:9-23; Rev. 14:11}*

¹⁰Standing afar off for the fear of her torment, saying, Alas, alas, that great city Babylon, that mighty city! for in one hour is thy judgment come.

Standing afar because of the fear of her four hidden dynasties' tormented condition, saying, Woe, woe, that great and mighty state of confusion! For in the hour of temptation (five-month period) your judgment came. *{Isa. 14:9-11; Zep. 3:8-9}*

¹¹And the merchants of the earth shall weep and mourn over her; for no man buyeth their merchandise any more:

And the merchants (including the perverse ministers and the Kenites) of the prince of this world age Satan, will grieve over her state of great confusion; because no one buys their load of false truths and mammon any longer:

When people discover and know the truth, they no longer fall for hypocrisy. At the start of the millennium when Christ returns, we are changed into our spiritual, breath of life bodies, and all will know the truth intuitively. Moreover, there will be no more commerce, idolatry, or covetousness for worldly possessions. The merchandise that no one will buy any longer is literal and figurative. *{Eze. 27:12-24; 1 Co. 15:49-55}*

¹²The merchandise of gold, and silver, and precious stones, and of pearls, and fine linen, and purple, and silk, and scarlet, and all thine wood, and all manner vessels of ivory, and all manner vessels of most precious wood, and of brass, and iron, and marble,

¹³And cinnamon, and odours, and ointments, and frankincense, and wine, and oil, and fine flour, and wheat, and beasts, and sheep, and horses, and chariots, and slaves, and souls of men.

All of the merchandise of mammon, heavy burdens, idols, and

religious systems of men, that appeared sacred to the eyes, sweet sounding to the ears, and sensual to the flesh, were designed to keep people enslaved to the ideologies and strong delusions of the harlot Satan, causing their souls to be hell bound.

This list consists of the four hidden dynasties (beast system), mammon, wanton luxuries, and idolatries, representing the vainglory that the unsuspecting and deceived people of the world covet after. Satan uses these dainty and worldly goods to reward those who assist in and execute his heresies and iniquities. In return, Satan seeks to capture the souls of men, attempting to seduce and destroy as many as he can from God. True servants of God and Christ store up treasures (spiritual gifts) in heaven which are eternal, not worldly treasures on earth which do rust and perish. *{Gen. 3:5-7; 1 Jo 2:15-17; Mat. 6:19-21}*

14*And the fruits that thy soul lusted after are departed from thee, and all things which were dainty and goodly are departed from thee, and thou shalt find them no more at all.*

And the forbidden fruits of covetousness that your soul desired are perished, and all worldly goods which were sumptuous and wanton are done away with, and men shall not find them ever again.

Upon Christ's Second Advent, when we enter into another dimension, worldly goods and luxuries are no longer of any value. *{Eze. 27:34-36; Rom. 1:28-32; 2 Pet. 3:10-12; 1 Jn. 2:15-18}*

15*The merchants of these things, which were made rich by her, shall stand afar off for the fear of her torment, weeping and wailing,*

The merchants (including the perverse ministers and the Kenites) of these things, who became enriched by her state of great confusion, will stand afar in fear of her four hidden dynasties' tormented condition, grieving and mourning, {Eze. 27:29-31}

^{16}And saying, Alas, alas, that great city, that was clothed in fine linen, and purple, and scarlet, and decked with gold, and precious stones, and pearls!

And saying, Woe! Woe to that great state of confusion which was arrayed as regal and sublime, having been adorned as the holy truth and righteousness of God! {Eze. 27:3-7}

^{17}For in one hour so great riches is come to nought. And every shipmaster, and all the company in ships, and sailors, and as many as trade by sea, stood afar off,

For within that five-month period all great wealth is made desolate. And every ship captain, and all company on the ships, and sailors, and all that trade for a living by sea, stood from afar,

The ceasing of commerce is not only literal, but also represents the ceasing of the spiritual trade of Satan's lies and deception. {Eze. 26:15-21, 28:1-19}

^{18}And cried when they saw the smoke of her burning, saying, What city is like unto this great city!

And cried out as they witnessed the smoke of the four hidden dynasties' destruction, saying, What state is like the state of great confusion? {Eze. 27:32}

^{19}And they cast dust on their heads, and cried, weeping

and wailing, saying, Alas, alas, that great city, wherein were made rich all that had ships in the sea by reason of her costliness! for in one hour is she made desolate.

And they lowered their heads in shame, and cried out, weeping and wailing, saying, Woe, woe, that great state of confusion, which enriched all that had ships in the sea through her splendor! For within the five-month period the four hidden dynasties are made desolate.

Trade and commerce is fueled by covetousness and lust for worldly possessions. Through Satan's four hidden dynasties, those who trade by sea for a living have been made very wealthy. *{Eze. 26:17, 27:30-31; Deu. 32:16-18; Isa. 46:8-15}*

[20] Rejoice over her, thou heaven, and ye holy apostles and prophets; for God hath avenged you on her.

Rejoice over the harlot Satan, you heavenly hosts and elect servants; for God YHVH has fully avenged you against her.

This verse documents the triumph and victory over Satan and his great deception for those who follow and execute the will and plan of God's Salvation in truth to the end. *{Isa. 14:15-18; Luk. 18:7-8}*

[21] And a mighty angel took up a stone like a great millstone, and cast it into the sea, saying, Thus with violence shall that great city Babylon be thrown down, and shall be found no more at all.

And a mighty angel lifted up the rock of Tyre as he were a great burden, and cast him into the abyss, saying, Thus with an outburst of wrath will that great state of confusion be destroyed, and will never rise again.

This stone, or rock of Tyre, is symbolic of Satan as the false rock who is a great and heavy burden upon the world. *{Exo. 15:4-5; Mar. 13:1-2; Jer. 23:28-32, 51:63-64; Eze. 26:21}*

²²And the voice of harpers, and musicians, and of pipers, and trumpeters, shall be heard no more at all in thee; and no craftsman, of whatsoever craft he be, shall be found anymore in thee; and the sound of a millstone shall be heard no more at all in thee;

And the utterance of inanimate things and confusion will no longer be heard from the harlot ministers; and every idol artificer, no matter the idol he crafts, will cease to exist; and the hardship of Satan's burdensome lies and blasphemies will no longer be heard from them;

The noise of babel, rapture theories, false doctrines, traditions, religion, and idol worship, that tickled the ears of the unsuspecting and biblically illiterate people of the world, will cease to exist. *{Deu. 32:31-33; Zec. 11:15-17; Isa. 56:10-12; Gen. 4:16-22}*

²³And the light of a candle shall shine no more at all in thee; and the voice of the bridegroom and of the bride shall be heard no more at all in thee: for thy merchants were the great men of the earth; for by thy sorceries were all nations deceived.

And the truth and wisdom of God was not found in the harlot ministers of Satan; neither was the testimony of Christ and His elect servants (with the seal of God) accepted and comprehended by hearing from them: for the merchants (including the perverse ministers and the Kenites) were the nobles and magnates of the world; and by their bewitchments and seductions of idolatry were all the nations led away into error and sin.

The perverse ministers and tyrants of the harlot Satan are no longer in the spotlight letting their persona and false truths shine. *{Jer. 16:9-13, 23:1-2; Isa. 9:13-17; Eze. 27; Mat. 5:14-16; Rev. 9:21}*

²⁴And in her was found the blood of prophets, and of saints, and of all that were slain upon the earth.

And it was discovered that the harlot Satan and his followers were guilty of murdering the prophets and the elect servants of God, and all those having been murdered on the earth.

The deceived religious community truly thought that they were doing the will of God, but in ignorance and unbelief they condemned and persecuted God's elect servants who witnessed and taught the truth of God and Christ Chapter by Chapter and verse by verse, which differed from their heretical, religious doctrines, traditions, and ideologies of men. *{Mat. 23:29-36; Isa. 47:1-15}*

Chapter 19

The Marriage of the Lamb

In Heaven

¹And after these things I heard a great voice of much people in heaven, saying, Alleluia; Salvation, and glory, and honour, and power, unto the LORD our God:

Afterward, I (John) heard the roar of a throng of people in heaven, saying, Praise you Yah! The salvation, the glory, and the power, belong to YHVH our God! *{Psa. 104:35; Zec. 13:9}*

²For true and righteous are His judgments: for He hath judged the great whore, which did corrupt the earth with her fornication, and hath avenged the blood of His servants at her hand.

Indeed, true and righteous are His judgments: because He has condemned the great harlot Satan, who defiled the world with idolatry, and He has avenged the murder of His elect servants at her hand. *{Eze. 28:17-19, Rev. 6:9-11}*

³And again they said, Alleluia. And her smoke rose up for ever and ever.

And a second time the people said, Praise you Yah! And the smoke of the harlot Satan's strong delusion ascended forever. *{Psa. 37:7, 20, 34}*

⁴And the four and twenty elders and the four beasts fell down and worshipped God That sat on the throne, saying, Amen; Alleluia.

And the twenty-four elders and the four living creatures fell prostrate and worshiped God YHVH, Who sits on the throne, saying, Of a truth! Praise you Yah!

⁵And a voice came out of the throne, saying, Praise our God, all ye His servants, and ye that fear Him, both small and great.

And a voice came out from the heavenly throne, saying, Praise our God YHVH, all of you His elect servants, and those who reverence Him, from the least to the greatest. *{Eze. 44:15, 28; Mat. 5:19-20}*

⁶And I heard as it were the voice of a great multitude, and as the voice of many waters, and as the voice of mighty thunderings, saying, Alleluia: for the LORD God Omnipotent reigneth.

And I heard the voice of the heavenly hosts as the sound of a throng of people, and the rumbling voices of Elohim (God), saying, Praise you Yah: because YHVH our God, The Omnipotent, reigns! *{Ex. 9:28; Jn. 17:3}*

⁷Let us be glad and rejoice, and give honour to Him: for the marriage of the Lamb is come, and His wife hath made herself ready.

Let us exult and be exceeding glad, and give the glory to Him: for the marriage festival of Christ Yasha`yah has arrived, and God's

Chapter 19: The Marriage of the Lamb

elect, His wife, have prepared themselves by staying a spiritual virgin. *{2 Co. 11:2-4; Mat. 5:11-12, 22:2-14; Zep. 3:19-20; Isa. 54:4-7, 62:5-7; Jer. 3:14; Mar. 13:17}*

> **⁸And to her was granted that she should be arrayed in fine linen, clean and white: for the fine linen is the righteousness of saints.**

And to the elect it was granted that they be arrayed in fine, bright and pure linen garments: indeed, the fine linen is the righteous acts of the saints. *{Psa. 45:13-15; Eze. 44:17-19; Lev. 16:4}*

> **⁹And he saith unto me, Write, Blessed are they which are called unto the marriage supper of the Lamb. And he saith unto me, These are the true sayings of God.**

And the angel said to me, Write, Happy are the ones who are invited to the marriage feast of Christ Yasha`yah. And he said to me, These are the true Words of God YHVH. *{Mat. 22:11-14}*

> **¹⁰And I fell at his feet to worship him. And he said unto me, see thou do it not: I am thy fellowservant, and of thy brethren that have the testimony of Jesus: worship God: for the testimony of Jesus is the spirit of prophecy.**

And I fell prostrate to worship at the feet of the angel messenger. And he rebuked me, saying, Do not worship me: I am your fellow servant, and of your brethren who heed the testimony of Christ Yasha`yah: worship God YHVH: indeed, the testimony of Christ Yasha`yah is the gift of communicating and enforcing revealed truth. *{Ex. 20:1-5; Am. 3:7-8}*

> **¹¹And I saw heaven opened, and behold, a white horse;**

and He that sat upon him was called Faithful and True, and in righteousness He doth judge and make war.

And I witnessed heaven having been opened, and beheld a white steed; and Christ Yasha`yah sitting thereon was called Faithful and True, and in righteousness He does condemn and decree warfare. *{Deu. 11:26-28; Jn. 16:23-28; Zec. 9:9-10; Mat. 21:4-11; 2 Co. 10:3-7; Rev. 2:16}*

¹²His eyes were as a flame of fire, and on His head were many crowns; and He had a name written, that no man knew, but He Himself.

And His being is the Holy Spirit of Truth, and upon His head the infinite majesty (kingship); and He has a name written on Him, which no one knows intuitively, except He Himself. The term *many crowns* is the exhibiting of Christ's omnipotence. No man knows the fullness and totality of God and Christ. *{Isa. 28:5-6; 2 Co. 3:17; Heb. 12:29}*

¹³And He was clothed with a vesture dipped in blood: and His name is called The Word of God.

And Christ Yasha`yah was clothed in a robe stained with the blood of His crucifixion: and His name is announced as The Living Word of God. *{Psa. 40:7-8; Jn. 1:1-5, 32-34, 3:16-21}*

¹⁴And the armies which were in heaven followed Him upon white horses, clothed in fine linen, white and clean.

And the heavenly hosts followed Christ Yasha`yah upon white steeds, having been arrayed in fine, bright and pure linen garments. *{2 Ths. 1:6-10; Jud. 14-15}*

CHAPTER 19: THE MARRIAGE OF THE LAMB

¹⁵And out of His mouth goeth a sharp sword, that with it He should smite the nations: and He shall rule them with a rod of iron: and He treadeth the winepress of the fierceness and wrath of Almighty God.

And out of the mouth of Christ Yasha`yah came forth the Living Truth of God with which to strike down the nations: and He will shepherd them with stern discipline: and He thrashes with an outburst of passion and the indignation of the Almighty God YHVH. *{Heb. 4:12; Psa. 2:7-9; Isa. 51:17-23, 63:2-3; Rev. 1:16, 14:20}*

¹⁶And He hath on His vesture and on His thigh a name written, KING OF KINGS, AND LORD OF LORDS.

And He had on His robe and on His thigh a vow having been written, KING OF KINGS, AND LORD OF LORDS.

This writing on the thigh is an oath which represents Christ Yasha`yah as being genuine, and the One and only Savior of humanity. *{Psa. 2:1-12; Eph. 6:13-17; Gen. 24:2-3, 9; Isa. 46:9; Col. 1:14-20}*

The Final Five Judgments

On Earth

¹⁷And I saw an angel standing in the sun; and he cried with a loud voice, saying to all the fowls that fly in the midst of heaven, Come and gather yourselves together unto the supper of the great God;

And I (John) saw the True, Bright Morning Star; and He shouted with a mighty voice to the entire angel host flying in mid-heaven, saying, Come, and be gathered together for the great supper of God YHVH;

This picnic battle will be against the harlot Satan and his evil band of followers. *{Eze. 39:17-22; Isa. 43:14-21; Luk. 22:27-30; Mat. 13:38-43}*

[18]*That ye may eat the flesh of kings, and the flesh of captains, and the flesh of mighty men, and the flesh of horses, and of them that sit on them, and the flesh of all men, both free and bond, both small and great.*

That you may devour all of the wicked entities of the world, regardless of status, from the least to the greatest.

It does not matter who you are or what title you hold in this second earth age; if you are seduced and have the seal of deception, you will be included in this group that is devoured. This event represents the cleansing of the earth from all wicked elements, and the condemnation of those corrupted with iniquity. *{1 Co. 6:2-3; Mat. 8:11-12; Eze. 39:17-22; 2 Pet. 3:10}*

[19]*And I saw the beast, and the kings of the earth, and their armies, gathered together to make war against Him that sat on the horse, and against His army.*

And I witnessed Satan's one-world government (beast system), and the rulers of the world, and their locust armies, gathered together to make war with Christ Yasha`yah sitting on the white steed, and with His angel hosts. *{Mat. 13:36-43; 2 Kgs. 6:14-18}*

²⁰And the beast was taken, and with him the false prophet that wrought miracles before him, with which he deceived them that had received the mark of the beast, and them that worshipped his image. These both were cast alive into a lake of fire burning with brimstone.

And Satan's one-world government was apprehended, along with his role as the Antichrist who performed miraculous acts of falsehood, by which he seduced the people that received his seal of deception, and worshiped his religious system. The two were cast alive into perdition and blotted out. *{Dan. 7:10-14; Isa. 43:27-28; 1 Pet. 4:17; Rev. 13, 20:10}*

²¹And the remnants were slain with the sword of Him that sat upon the horse, which sword proceeded out of His mouth: and all the fowls were filled with their flesh.

And the rest of the deceived mortal souls were killed spiritually (deprived of immortality) with the Living Truth of Christ Yasha`yah, which came forth out of His mouth: and all of the saints of God and Christ were avenged against their enemies. *{Isa. 1:20, 61:1-4; Luk. 21:22-23}*

Chapter 20

The Millennium

On Earth

¹And I saw an angel come down from heaven, having the key of the bottomless pit and a great chain in his hand.

And I (John) witnessed Michael, the mighty archangel, descending from heaven, holding the key to the pit of the Abyss and a great chain in his hand. *{Rev. 12:7-9; 2 Ths. 2:7-8}*

²And he laid hold on the dragon, that old serpent, which is the Devil, and Satan, and bound him a thousand years,

And he seized the great serpent, that ancient serpent from the Garden of Eden, who is the Devil, and the Adversary (Satan), and bound him physically and spiritually for one thousand years (i.e. the millennium),

The ancient serpent Satan who brought about sin, death, and misery to the world, will be confined during the millennium, having no influence; but he will return as the Warlord for the final testing of the mortal souls, and be cast into perdition. *{Rev. 17:8, 11; Eze. 44:23-27; Isa. 14:16-17}*

³And cast him in to the bottomless pit, and shut him up,

and set a seal upon him, that he should deceive the nations no more, till the thousand years should be fulfilled: and after that he must be loosed a little season.

And threw Satan into the pit of the Abyss, and shut it and sealed it over him, prohibiting him from having any deceptive influence over the mortal souls until the Day of the Lord (millennium) is fulfilled: after these things he will be released for a short time.

On the Day of the Lord, the millennium, those who were seduced by Satan as the Antichrist will be sternly taught discipline by God's elect servants, without the influence of Satan's lies and deception. After this, Satan is released as the Warlord for the final testing of those mortal souls who failed to overcome him in this second earth age. {Jn. 16:33; 2 Pet. 3:5-10}

⁴And I saw thrones, and they sat upon them, and judgment was given unto them; and I saw the souls of them that were beheaded for the witness of Jesus, and for the Word of God, and which had not worshipped the beast, neither his image, neither had received his mark upon their foreheads, or in their hands; and they lived and reigned with Christ a thousand years.

And I witnessed the Father YHVH, Christ Yasha`yah, and the elect angels, as assessors sitting on thrones, and awards of honor were given to them. And I saw the souls of those who had been beheaded because of their testimony of Christ Yasha`yah and because of teaching the truth of God's Word, and those who had not worshiped the beast Satan as the Antichrist, or his religious system, neither received his seal of deception in their minds, nor participated in his evil works; and they received immortality and reigned with Christ Yasha`yah a thousand years. *{Rev. 1:4, 3:21; 1 Tim. 5:21; 2 Pet. 3:5-10; Mat. 10:28, 19:28, 25:31-34}*

> **⁵But the rest of the dead lived not again until the thousand years were finished. This is the first resurrection.**

The rest of the spiritually dead, deceived mortal souls were not able to receive immortality until the thousand-year period was fulfilled. This is the first resurrection. *{1 Co. 15:50-57}*

> **⁶Blessed and holy is he that hath part in the first resurrection: on such the second death hath no power, but they shall be priests of God and of Christ, and shall reign with Him a thousand years.**

Happy and holy is the one taking part in the first resurrection: over these the perishing of the soul has no authority, but they will be priests of God YHVH and Christ Yasha`yah, and will reign with Christ a thousand years. *{1 Ths. 4:13-17; Eze. 44:15, 16, 23-26; 2 Co. 5:6-10}*

> **⁷And when the thousand years are expired, Satan shall be loosed out of his prison,**

And when the thousand years are fulfilled, Satan as the Warlord will be released from his imprisonment,

Satan is released for the final test on the mortal souls whom he initially seduced while in his disguise as the Christ of God.

⁸And shall go out to deceive the nations which are in the four quarters of the earth, Gog and Magog, to gather them together to battle: the number of whom is as the sand of the sea.

And will go out to seduce the nations of mortal souls around the world, from east to west, gathering them to the war predicted and determined: the number of them being innumerable.

Those who do not take heed to the stern discipline of God's elect servants, but choose to follow Satan again this time around, are deserving of their sentence to be cast into perdition and blotted to ashes. *{Eze. 38, 39; Heb. 11:12}*

⁹And they went up on the breadth of the earth, and compassed the camp of the saints about, and the beloved city: and fire came down from God out of heaven, and devoured them.

And they marched up over the span of the earth as an army in line for battle, surrounding the sanctuary of the saints and the beloved city of Jerusalem: and the fire of God came down out of heaven, and utterly consumed them.

Satan and his evil band of followers are defeated once again, and those who fought with Satan are now thrown into Hades (hell) to await their final judgment of damnation. *{Eze. 44:23-27; Dan. 7:18, 27; Isa. 30:27, 60:12}*

¹⁰And the devil that deceived them was cast into the lake of fire and brimstone, where the beast and the false prophet are, and shall be tormented day and night for ever and ever.

CHAPTER 20: THE MILLENNIUM

And Satan the devil, which seduced the mortal souls, was cast into perdition, where his one-world government and role as the Antichrist were also cast; and they were blotted to ashes.

Satan's one-world government and his disguise as the spurious messiah Antichrist, were already cast into perdition, and now it is his time to be blotted to ashes and never exist again. {Dan. 7:11; Eze. 28:18-19; Rev. 19:20}

¹¹And I saw a great white throne, and Him that sat on it, from Whose face the earth and the heaven fled away; and there was found no place for them.

And I saw a great, holy and righteous throne, and God YHVH sitting upon it, from Whose appearance this second earth and heaven age and all wicked elements therein perished forever. {2 Pet. 3:10-13}

¹²And I saw the dead, small and great, stand before God; and the books were opened: and another book was opened, which is the book of life: and the dead were judged out of those things which were written in the books, according to their works.

And I saw the spiritually dead, mortal souls of the second resurrection, from the least to the greatest, standing before the great, holy and righteous throne of God; and the book of judgment and the Lamb's book of eternal life were opened: and the mortal souls were judged from the things having been written in the books, according to their works. {Mat. 5:19; Rev. 20:5}

¹³And the sea gave up the dead which were in it; and death and hell delivered up the dead which

were in them: and they were judged every man according to their works.

And the masses delivered up the mortal souls who were among them; and death and Hades delivered up the mortal souls that were in them: and they were judged individually according to their works.

The mortal souls that the masses deliver up for judgment are those that after being taught discipline in the millennium, chose not to follow Satan again during his final crusade. They are called the dead because they did not overcome at the first resurrection, and cannot receive immortality until they are judged and deserving. The mortal souls that were delivered up from Hades were there awaiting their sentence of perdition because they still chose to follow Satan, fighting against Christ and His saints. {Isa. 24:21-23}

¹⁴And death and hell were cast into the lake of fire. This is the second death.

And death and Hades were blotted out forever. This is the final death, the perishing of the soul. {1 Co. 15:54-57; Mat. 25:41; Heb. 2:14}

¹⁵And whosoever was not found written in the book of life was cast into the lake of fire.

And if anyone was not found written in the Lamb's book of eternal life, he was cast into perdition, to be blotted to ashes. {Dan. 7:9-10; Mat. 13:40-43; Rev. 21:8}

Chapter 21

The Description of the Heavenly Jerusalem and the People on the Rejuvenated Earth

¹And I saw a new heaven and a new earth: for the first heaven and the first earth were passed away; and there was no more sea.

Afterward, I (John) saw a rejuvenated heaven and earth age: indeed the former heaven and earth age had passed away; and there was no longer any sea.

The first heaven and earth age having been deluged with water, perished, and this second earth age will be destroyed by the fervent heat of the Holy Spirit (fire) of God. In the third heaven and earth age to come, there is no new earth, but a rejuvenated earth where all oceans and seas are dried up and returned back into the firmament. Moreover, the flood that destroyed the first earth age is not Noah's flood, but the immense flood after the overthrow and fall of Lucifer, Satan the devil, at his rebellion. *{Zech. 9:10; Jer. 4:23-27; Gen. 1:6-10; Isa. 42:15, 51:15-16, 65:17; 2 Pet. 3:3-13}*

²And I John saw the holy city, new Jerusalem, coming down from God out of heaven, prepared as a bride

adorned for her husband.

And I witnessed the holy city, the heavenly Jerusalem, descending out of heaven from God, having been prepared as a bride adorned for her Husband. *{Gal. 4:26; Jer. 33:15-16; Eze. 16:1-13; Isa. 52; Heb. 12:22-23}*

³*And I heard a great voice out of heaven saying, Behold, the tabernacle of God is with men, and He will dwell with them, and they shall be His people, and God Himself shall be with them, and be their God.*

And I heard a mighty voice from the throne saying, Behold, the dwelling of Immanuel (God with us) is with His people Israel, and He will tabernacle with them, and the "sheep" nations (of His right hand) will be His peoples, and YHVH Himself will be with them as their God. *{Mat. 25:31-46; Rev. 21:24; Isa. 7:14; Eze. 48:35; Hos. 1:9-11; Zec. 2:10-11, 8:3-8; Ex. 29:45-46}*

⁴*And God shall wipe away all tears from their eyes; and there shall be no more death, neither sorrow, nor crying, neither shall there be any more pain: for the former things are passed away.*

And God YHVH will wipe away every tear from their eyes; and death will be no more, neither mourning, nor weeping, neither will there be any more anguish: indeed the former things have ceased to exist. *{Jer. 31:12-14}*

⁵*And He that sat upon the throne said, Behold, I make all things new. And He said unto me, Write: for these words are true and faithful.*

Chapter 21: The Description of the Heavenly Jerusalem...

And God YHVH, Who sits on the throne, said, Behold, I make all things rejuvenated. And He said, Write: indeed these words are faithful and true. *{Eze. 44:15-30}*

⁶And He said unto me, It is done. I am Alpha and Omega, the Beginning and the End. I will give unto him that is athirst of the fountain of the water of life freely.

And He said to me, They are come to pass! I Am that I Am, the Beginning of life and the Ending of death. To the one thirsting, I will freely give of the spring of the water of eternal life. *{Jn. 4:10, 14; Rev. 16:17}*

⁷He that overcometh shall inherit all things; and I will be his God, and he shall be My son.

The one overcoming Satan will inherit these things; and I will be his God, and he will be My son. *{Eze. 44:15-16, 23-31; Isa. 61:9-11}*

⁸But the fearful, and unbelieving, and the abominable, and murderers, and whoremongers, and sorcerers, and idolaters, and all liars, shall have their part in the lake which burneth with fire and brimstone; which is the second death.

But to the cowardly, and faithless, having become abominable, and murderers, and the sexually immoral, and religious incantators, and idolaters, and all the false, will take part in perdition; which is the perishing of the soul. *{Rom. 2:22-23; Zec. 13:2-3; Mat. 10:28; Isa. 30:33; Pro. 6:16-19}*

⁹And there came unto me one of the seven angels

which had the seven vials full of the seven last plagues, and talked with me, saying, Come hither, I will show thee the bride, the Lamb's wife.

And one of the seven angels, having the seven broad, shallow cups full of God's indignation, came and spoke to me, saying, Come here, I will show you the bride, Christ Yasha`yah's wife.

This bride as Christ Yasha`yah's wife is Israel of the heavenly calling of the new holy Jerusalem. *{Eze. 37:15-28; Heb. 3:1, 11:13-16}*

¹⁰And he carried me away in the spirit to a great and high mountain, and showed me that great city, the holy Jerusalem, descending out of heaven from God,

And he carried me away in the Spirit to a glorious and exalted nation, and showed me the holy city Jerusalem, descending out of heaven from God YHVH, *{Jer. 3:17; Eze. 1:1, 37:22-28}*

¹¹Having the glory of God: and her light was like unto a stone most precious, even like a jasper stone, clear as crystal;

Having the Shekhinah Glory of God YHVH: and the radiance of her was like the expressed image of the most precious Rock, Christ Yasha`yah, being most holy and pure; *{Deu. 32:3-4}*

¹²And had a wall great and high, and had twelve gates, and at the gates twelve angels, and names written thereon, which are the names of the twelve tribes of the children of Israel:

And had a vast and lofty wall, having twelve gates, and guardian angels at each gate, and names having been inscribed, which are the names of the twelve tribes of the sons of Israel: *{Eze. 48:31-35}*

¹³On the east three gates; on the north three gates; on the south three gates; and on the west three gates.

On the east were three gates; on the north three gates; on the south three gates; and on the west three gates. *{Zec. 14:4-5}*

¹⁴And the wall of the city had twelve foundations, and in them the names of the twelve apostles of the Lamb.

And the wall of the holy city Jerusalem had twelve foundation stones, and engraved on them were the twelve names of the twelve apostles of Christ Yasha`yah. *{Acts 1:11-13; Rev. 3:12; Pro. 9:1}*

¹⁵And he that talked with me had a golden reed to measure the city, and the gates thereof, and the wall thereof.

The angel who spoke with me had a gold measuring rod to measure out the city, and its gates, and its wall.

¹⁶And the city lieth foursquare, and the length is as large as the breadth: and he measured the city with the reed, twelve thousand furlongs. The length and the breadth and the height of it are equal.

The city was laid out as a square, and its length is the same as the width: and he measured the holy city with the rod, fifteen hundred miles; its length, width and height are equal. *{Zec. 2:1-5}*

¹⁷And he measured the wall thereof, an hundred and forty and four cubits, according to the measure of a man, that is, of the angel.

And he measured its wall, seventy-two yards, according to human measurements, which are also angelic measurements. *{Eze. 43:13}*

¹⁸And the building of the wall of it was of jasper: and the city was pure gold, like unto clear glass.

The material of the wall was jasper: and the city was most sacred, holy and pure.

This symbolizes the holy city Jerusalem as heaven on earth and as being the perfect place to be inhabited and reside. The city being pure gold is not a matter of riches, but of purity, sanctification and sacredness.

¹⁹And the foundations of the wall of the city were garnished with all manner of precious stones. The first foundation was jasper; the second, sapphire; the third, a chalcedony; the fourth, an emerald;

²⁰The fifth, sardonyx; the sixth, sardius; the seventh, chrysolyte; the eighth, beryl; the ninth, a topaz; the tenth, a chrysoprasus; the eleventh, a jacinth; the twelfth, an amethyst.

The foundation stones of the city wall were adorned with every kind of precious stone. The first foundation stone was jasper; the second, sapphire; the third, chalcedony; the fourth, emerald; the fifth, onyx; the sixth, carnelian; the seventh, chrysolite; the eighth, beryl; the ninth, topaz; the tenth, chrysoprase; the eleventh, jacinth; the twelfth, amethyst.

The twelve stones represent the twelve tribes of Israel and the stones in Aaron's breastplate as the high priest, and it also denotes governmental perfection. *{Eze. 37:21-28; Ex. 28:17-21; Isa. 54:11-12}*

²¹And the twelve gates were twelve pearls; every several gate was of one pearl: and the street of the city was pure gold, as it was transparent glass.

And the twelve gates were made of twelve pearls; respectively, each one of the gates was of one pearl: and the city street was holy and pure.

The street is not made of glass, but of gold of a kind unknown to man. Twelve in biblical numeric denotes governmental perfection. The kingdom of God on earth is the perfect governmental system where there is divine unity and justice. *{Mat. 6:9-10; Zec. 8:3-8; 2 Pet. 3:10}*

²²And I saw no Temple therein: for the LORD God Almighty and the Lamb are the Temple of it.

And I (John) saw no Temple building in the holy city: indeed YHVH God Almighty and Christ Yasha`yah are its Temple.

No man-made building or sanctuary can compare to God YHVH Almighty and Christ Yasha`yah. *{Zec. 14:9; Eze. 37:27-28, 48:35; Mar. 14:58; Mat. 18:20; Isa. 2:2-3}*

²³And the city had no need of the sun, neither of the

moon, to shine in it: for the glory of God did lighten it, and the Lamb is the light thereof.

And the holy city needed no light from the sun or of the moon to shine on her: indeed the Shekhinah Glory of God YHVH illuminated her and Christ Yasha`yah is the Illumination (spiritual enlightenment) of her. *{Gen. 1:2-4; Heb. 1:1-3; John 1:1-9, 3:16-21, 10:30; Isa. 11:6-9, 60:17-22}*

²⁴ And the nations of them which are saved shall walk in the light of it: and the kings of the earth do bring their glory and honour into it.

And the "sheep" nations (of His right hand) will walk in the divine truth and knowledge of Christ Yasha`yah: and the elect of the nations will bring the glory (love) of their nations into the holy city Jerusalem. *{Mat. 25:31-46; Isa. 14:1, 60:1-3, 10-16; Hab. 2:14; Jn. 3:18-21; 2 Chr. 20:21-26; Joe. 3:1-2}*

²⁵ And the gates of it shall not be shut at all by day: for there shall be no night there.

And the gates of her will never be shut at all during the day: indeed there will be no nighttime there.

It will always remain daylight and peaceful because the prince of darkness Satan, his followers, and all evil elements, are utterly consumed. *{Zec. 14:7; Isa. 60:11-12}*

²⁶ And they shall bring the glory and honour of the nations into it.

And the elect of the "sheep" nations will bring the glory

CHAPTER 21: THE DESCRIPTION OF THE HEAVENLY JERUSALEM...

and the honor of their nations into the holy city Jerusalem. *{Zep. 3:19-20; Mat. 25:31-46}*

²⁷And there shall in no wise enter into it any thing that defileth, neither whatsoever worketh abomination, or maketh a lie: but they which are written in the Lamb's book of life.

And anything that is defiled (unclean) will by no means enter into the holy city Jerusalem, neither anyone who practices a lying abomination: except for those having been written in Christ Yasha`yah's book of eternal life. *{Zep. 3:17-20}*

Chapter 22

The Conclusion of the Tree of Life

On Earth

¹And he showed me a pure river of water of life, clear as crystal, proceeding out of the throne of God and of the Lamb.

And the angel showed me a river of living water, clear as crystal, flowing out of the throne of God YHVH and of Christ Yasha`yah. *{Eze. 47:1-13; Zec. 6:13; Jn. 4:10-14}*

²In the midst of the street of it, and on either side of the river, was there the tree of life, which bare twelve manner of fruits, and yielded her fruit every month: and the leaves of the tree were for the healing of the nations.

In the middle of its street, and on both sides of the river, was the Tree of Life (Christ the Living Word), bearing twelve kinds of fruit, yielding its fruit (for the enjoyment of the citizens of the new Jerusalem) according to each month; and the leaves of the tree are for the healing of the nations. *{Eze. 47:1-5, 12; Gen. 3:22-24; Luk. 23:31; Rev. 21:4}*

³And there shall be no more curse: but the throne of God

and of the Lamb shall be in it; and His servants shall serve Him;

And there will be no longer an accursed thing: and the throne of God YHVH and Christ Yasha`yah will exist in the holy city Jerusalem; and His elect servants will serve Him; *{Jos. 7:1, 11-15, 20-21; Rev. 4:11; Col. 1:16-17; Zec. 14:11}*

⁴And they shall see His face; and His name shall be in their foreheads.

And they will discern perfectly His nature, will, and purposes; and His seal will be in their minds. *{Hab. 2:14}*

⁵And there shall be no night there; and they need no candle, neither light of the sun; for the LORD God giveth them light: and they shall reign for ever and ever.

And there will no longer be any night; and they will not have need of the light of a lamp, nor the light of the sun; because God YHVH will illumine them: and they will reign with Him for an eternity.

The reign of the saints with Christ the Messiah is for a thousand years; and the reign here with God YHVH is forever and ever. *{Jn. 11:9-10; Eze. 44:27-28; Isa. 60:19-20}*

⁶And he said unto me, These sayings are faithful and true: and the LORD God of the holy prophets sent His angel to show unto His servants the things which must shortly be done.

Chapter 22: The Conclusion of the Tree of Life

And the angel said to me, These words are faithful and true: and the YHVH, the God of the spirits of the prophets, sent His messenger to show to His elect servants the things which will soon come to pass. {Zec. 8:9; Am. 3:7-8; Mat. 20:16; Rom. 8:26-39, 10:13-15}

⁷Behold, I come quickly: blessed is he that keepeth the sayings of the prophecy of this book.

And behold, I am coming suddenly. Blessed is he who heeds the words of the prophecy of this book. {2 Pet. 3:10-12}

⁸And I John saw these things, and heard them. And when I had heard and seen, I fell down to worship before the feet of the angel which showed me these things.

I, John, am he that heard and saw these things. And when I heard and saw, I fell prostrate to worship at the feet of the angel who showed me these things. {Rev. 1:1-2}

⁹Then saith he unto me, See thou do it not: for I am thy fellowservant, and of thy brethren the prophets, and of them which keep the sayings of this book: worship God.

And he said to me, Do not do that. I am a fellow servant of yours, and of your brethren the prophets, and of those who heed the words of this book: Worship God YHVH. {Ex. 20:1-6}

¹⁰And he saith unto me, Seal not the sayings of the prophecy of this book; for the time is at hand.

And he said to me, Do not conceal the words of the prophecy of this book; indeed the time is near.

¹¹He that is unjust, let him be unjust still: and he which is filthy, let him be filthy still: and he that is righteous, let him be righteous still: and he that is holy, let him be holy still.

The one being unrighteous, let him act unrighteous still: and he who is immoral, let him remain immoral still: and he who is righteous, let him practice righteousness still; and he who is sanctified, let him remain sanctified still.

Only God YHVH and His Living Word, Christ Yasha`yah, can truly change lives for the better. Therefore, remain faithful and true, and plant the seeds of truth and righteousness from God's word to those who are biblically illiterate and unsuspecting. *{2 Ths. 3:13-15; 1 Co. 14:38}*

¹²And behold, I come quickly; and My reward is with Me, to give every man according as his work shall be.

Behold, I am coming suddenly; and My reward is with Me, to render to each person as his (or her) work is. *{1 Chr. 28:9-10; Am. 8:7; Ecc. 12:14; 2 Co. 5:1-10}*

¹³I am Alpha and Omega, the Beginning and the End, the First and the Last.

I am the Alpha and the Omega, the First and the Last, the Beginning (of life) and the End (of death). *{Ex. 3:14-15}*

¹⁴Blessed are they that do His commandments, that they may have right to the tree of life, and may enter in through the gates into the city.

CHAPTER 22: THE CONCLUSION OF THE TREE OF LIFE

Blessed are those who wash their robes (by executing God's righteous judgement and peace), so that they may have the right to the Tree of Life (Christ), and may enter by the gates into the holy city Jerusalem. *{Eze. 45:9; Zec. 8:16-17; Gen. 3:22-24; Deu. 33:29; Eph. 5:25-27; Rev. 4:11}*

¹⁵For without are dogs, and sorcerers, and whoremongers, and murderers, and idolaters, and whosoever loveth and maketh a lie.

But outside are the abominable ones (Sodomites), and the religious incantators, and the sexually immoral, and the murderers, and the idolaters, and everyone loving and practicing falsehood. *{Rom. 1:24-32; 1 Sam. 15:23; Deu. 23:17-18; Ecc. 12:14; Phn. 3:2; 2 Pet. 2:22; Rev. 21:8}*

¹⁶I Jesus have sent Mine angel to testify unto you these things in the churches. I am the Root and the Offspring of David, and the bright and morning Star.

I Christ Yasha`yah have sent My messenger to testify to you these things concerning the churches (that He found well pleasing). I Am the root and the descendant of David (through the flesh, of the tribe of Judah), the True, Bright Morning Star. *{Rev. 2:8-10, 3:7-10; Mat. 1:1, 22:41-45; Num. 24:17; Isa. 14:12}*

¹⁷And the Spirit and the bride say, Come. And let him that heareth say, Come. And let him that is athirst come. And whosoever will, let him take the water of life freely.

The Holy Spirit and the elect of God and Christ say, Come! And let the one hearing with spiritual understanding say, Come! And let the one thirsting for God's truth and knowledge come; let the one desiring, take the Living Word of God and Christ freely (without cost). *{Jn. 7:37-39; Pro. 1:7, 2:5-7; 1 Co. 2:13; 2 Tim. 3:16; 2 Pet. 1:21; Mat. 5:6, 22:2-14}*

¹⁸For I testify unto every man that heareth the words of the prophecy of this book, If any man shall add unto these things, God shall add unto him the plagues that are written in this book:

Indeed I (Christ) testify to everyone who hears with understanding the words prophesied in this book, If anyone adds to them, God will add to him the plagues having been written in this book (of the Bible):

The Word of God is all-inclusive; theories, myths and traditions of men should never be added. *{Deu. 4:1-2, 28:15-45; Num. 14:36-37; 2 Ths. 10-12; Gal. 3:10}*

¹⁹And if any man shall take away from the words of the book of this prophecy, God shall take away his part out of the book of life, and out of the holy city, and from the things which are written in this book.

And if anyone should take away from the words of the book of this prophecy, God will take away his inheritance from the Tree of Life (Christ), and out of the holy city Jerusalem, and from the blessings having been written in this book (of the Bible). *{Deu. 12:32; Hag. 1:5-11; Eze. 13:16-23; Pro. 30:5-6}*

²⁰He Which testifieth these things saith, Surely I come quickly. Amen. Even so, come, Lord Jesus.

The One testifying to these things says, Yes, I am coming

suddenly. So be it, come, Lord Yasha`yah. *{2 Co. 1:19-20}*

²¹The grace of our Lord Jesus Christ be with you all. Amen.

The grace of the Lord Christ Yasha`yah be with all the righteous ones (saints). So be it.

The Reality of Revelation, Unveiled

Biography

Michael A. Riles was born and raised in Dallas, Texas, and introduced to Christianity as a young child by his family. Called by the Lord in April 1995, Michael began a personal and profound journey one afternoon while meditating about God's master plan and intended purpose for him and others on this earth. He wondered why some are blessed, while others seem to suffer. Contemplating this and other questions about the greater good and deeper meaning of life, Michael turned to the Bible for guidance and direction.

Fervent study, research, prayer, and faith in the Holy Spirit enabled Michael to mature spiritually. He found peace and comfort in the ways of the LORD and through His Word's many lessons, all of which gave him new knowledge and wisdom in his search for the truth. By studying the Word of God as written in the Greek and Hebrew languages, he gained new biblical insight, unfettered by the multitude of religious doctrines that exist.

With his unwavering drive for learning and spiritual growth, Michael earned a teaching certificate from the Evangelical Training Association, and an honorary Doctor of Divinity and Doctor of Philosophy in Biblical Studies. He continues his commitment to further his knowledge and spiritual understanding in God's great Word.

As a spiritual counselor and ordained minister of the LORD and His Savior Christ Yasha`yah, Michael today teaches with a commitment to helping those who are finding again, or for the first time, the truth in God's Word.

Dr. Michael A. Riles is available for speaking engagements and personal appearances. For more information contact:

Michael A. Riles
C/O Advantage Books
PO Box 160847
Altamonte Springs, FL 32779

info@advbooks.com

To purchase additional copies of this book or other books published by Advantage Books call our toll free order number at:
407-788-3110 (Book Orders Only)

or visit our bookstore website at:
www.advbookstore.com

Longwood, Florida, USA
"we bring dreams to life"™
www.advbooks.com

www.ingramcontent.com/pod-product-compliance
Lightning Source LLC
Chambersburg PA
CBHW060530100426
42743CB00009B/1476